BOWS & ARROWS
OF THE
NATIVE AMERICANS

BOWS & ARROWS
OF THE
NATIVE AMERICANS

A Complete Step-by-Step Guide to
Wooden Bows, Sinew-backed Bows,
Composite Bows, Strings, Arrows & Quivers

JIM HAMM

The Lyons Press

In cooperation with
BOIS d'ARC PRESS

The Lyons Press is an imprint of The Globe Pequot Press.

11 12 13 14 15

Library of Congress Cataloging-in-Publication Data is available on file.

ISBN: 1-55821-168-3

PICTURE CREDITS

Front cover: Buffalo horn bow like was used on the Northern Plains ca. 1830.
Back cover: Quilled otter quiver and bowcase for buffalo horn bow.
Cover photos by Mary Ann Fittipaldi.
All other photos by Jim or Donna Hamm unless otherwise noted.
Graphics Production—LeWay Composing Service, Inc., Fort Worth, Texas.

ACKNOWLEDGEMENTS

My warmest thanks to Carney Saupitty Sr. and Bill Crawford, two weapons makers from the old school who have handed some of their knowledge down to me.

Lynda Roper, with the Ft. Sill, Oklahoma Archives, went beyond the call of duty.

Thanks to Pam Taylor, who provided editorial assistance.

Scott Silsby gave me the nice stone ax pictured on page 12.

My wife, Donna, has contributed valuable insights to this book, along with some fine craftwork. Her help and support is what makes this possible as well as fun.

DEDICATION

To Brad and Buford who went before,
To Lee and Reed who are coming after.

CONTENTS

CONTENTS *Continued*

FOREWORD

I'm a hunter. Just like my ancestors were, and yours too for that matter, at some point in the past. Maybe their influence explains why I spend so much time hunting, making traditional weapons, or thinking about making weapons. Any kind of hunting is fine with me, but I especially love to go after whitetail deer with a bow. That's why I originally started making bows years ago.

After hunting deer and turkeys with a rifle since I was a kid, there reached the point where it was no longer a challenge. If you can shoot at all, killing a deer inside of two hundred yards is not hard with a .308 and 6 power scope. I started hunting with a muzzleloader. More difficult, but with an accurate range of at least a hundred yards it was still too easy. I wanted to see the whites of their eyes. So I started using a bow.

Wanting to hunt with a bow, but wanting to use a natural, traditional bow instead of a store-bought block and tackle bow, I was forced to make my own since no one had wooden bows and flint-tipped arrows for sale. The idea of hunting with weapons that have been used for five thousand years appealed to me. I wanted to match wits with the animal directly, without a lot of gadgets and machinery in the way. Perhaps again, the imprint from my distant, bloody ancestors.

Anyway, since there was very little accurate, detailed information on how to construct old-time, Indian-style weapons, I started making them by the trial and error method. Emphasis on the error. The first fifteen bows broke. Since persistence is one of my rare virtues (my wife would substitute bull-headed), I pushed grimly ahead. Slowly the mistakes were cured and I began turning out nice, serviceable weapons that could be used for hunting, which is what had started this epic tale to begin with.

Once the bow and arrow-making was perfected, a few friends and acquaintances asked me to construct weapons for them. Since they insisted on paying for my time and expertise with hard United States currency, I was glad to oblige. It occurred to me that other people might be interested in these traditional bows and arrows, too, so I placed a few small ads in magazines. One thing led to another, and over time I had orders from all over the world and was doing interviews for newspapers and magazines. To make a long story short, I wound up doing this for a living.

After making a couple of hundred bows and a few thousand arrows, I wrote and starred (??!) in a video on how to make traditional weapons. The feedback from folks around the country has been uplifting and humbling. Hundreds have begun making bows, adding to the people that are helping to keep this once vanishing art alive. They are also delving into areas that I had neither the time, nor inclination, to explore and are now passing along their discoveries to me and others.

Many people have suggested, asked, and occasionally insisted that this book be written. Now that it's a reality, I hope it will be a catalyst for others to get started and will save someone, maybe you, from all the stupid mistakes I made when I began. Hopefully, with this book, the first bow you make will be a shooter.

The bows and arrows I describe will be traditional in every way, a result of weeks spent in museum storage areas taking thousands of pictures and measurements. I've also invested years perfecting the traditional methods outlined

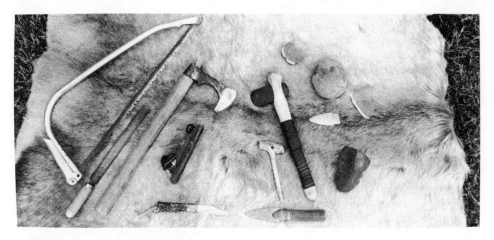

in this book. With that said, be advised that you may find better ways to do something, or may be able to incorporate these methods into your own. Use this book as a starting point, since all of the techniques described herein work, but don't be afraid to try something different or even radically opposed to my methods once you get started and understand the basics. I wrote the book, in a manner of speaking, but don't necessarily have all the answers.

Purists may complain that this book is not about how to sit under a bush and laboriously fashion a bow and arrows with stone-age tools. With the theory that you have to crawl before you can walk, and since we don't have elders steeped in five thousand years of weapons-making looking over our shoulders, I have chosen to show how to make bows and arrows the easiest way, with steel tools. If a beginning bowyer was going to make mistakes, I felt it was better to make them on a bow in which he had invested thirty hours rather than on a bow he had spent a hundred hours scraping with flint chips. Once the basic techniques are mastered, one can always begin using stone tools, if one's so inclined.

You'll notice, in the text, that I've adroitly covered myself by using qualifiers such as 'usually,' 'sometimes,' 'normally,' and 'in most cases.' One learns through experience not to make flat, all-encompassing statements concerning Indian people or their ways. Never say never. And never say always. A Native American, or an observant student of Indian people and their history, can no doubt still find some exceptions to the generalizations in this book. That's to be expected.

A final word on how I approach the making of bows and arrows. I've found the going much smoother when I looked upon the wood and stone and sinew and feathers with respect as fellow living things rather than just as raw materials. Work with the wood, rather than trying to impose too much of your will upon it. Understand that you're taking all of these unrelated things and through your skill are transforming them into a deadly weapon. If you choose to take this weapon and hunt with it and perhaps make a kill, you will have come full circle, back to our ancestors who passed this wonder art down to us . . .

Jim Hamm
Mill Creek, Republic of Texas
Fall, 1989

Part 1

BOWS

When we talk about "primitive" bows and arrows, most people have thoughts of crude implements, rudely fashioned and ineffective. There is an image of crooked bows and moth-eaten arrows as are often seen in museums. Compared to modern compound bows shooting aluminum arrows with plastic fletching, a primitive bow seems almost like a child's toy.

After considering that our ancestors lived for thousands of years by taking the biggest and most dangerous game imaginable with their arrows, the image of childish weapons fades a bit. The image further fades as we reflect that most museum pieces were collected after years of hard use and have been abused for all of the time since then. Museum bows have been left strung, strung backwards, overdrawn, stood in a corner, and unoiled in a hundred and fifty years. It's doubtful if the best compound on the market today would be in shooting condition a hundred and fifty years from now if subjected to the same misuse. After looking beyond the rough treatment and age of museum pieces, we usually see carefully made wooden bows, or composite bows made from horn and sinew, or painstakingly made sets of arrows. It's only when attempting to recreate these pieces that we finally begin to appreciate how patient, skilled, innovative, and artistic the old-time masters of this craft really were.

Traditional or primitive to me simply means that the bows and arrows are made from natural materials and does not reflect upon their beauty or utility. These same natural materials are still available and we are able to recreate the weapons that effectively kept our ancestors fed.

A BRIEF LESSON IN BOW PHYSICS

A piece of wood must absorb a lot of punishment when made into a bow. As a bow is bent, the wood is subjected to two powerful, but opposite, forces. The back of the bow is being stretched, undergoing tension, while the belly of the bow is being compressed, or crushed. When a bow is overdrawn, it breaks, usually from the back where the wood pulls apart, but sometimes on the belly when the wood suffers compression fractures, or becomes crystallized.

Ancient bowyers came up with two remarkable innovations to allow them to draw a wooden bow further, or conversely, to pull a given length arrow in a shorter bow. The first, and most widely used innovation, was sinew backing. Animal sinew has a wonderful ability to stretch, and when glued to the back of a bow, will stretch tighter the further the bow is pulled. This tightly stretched layer of sinew holds down the wooden fibers on the back of a bow and doesn't give the bow a place to start breaking. Modern fiberglass accomplishes much the same thing but sinew holds one big advantage over it. As mentioned, sinew stretches, so with its great elasticity will snap back to shape when an arrow is released. The added tension of the sinew greatly improves the speed with which a bow can propel an arrow.

The other improvement in bowmaking was the composite bow, but it was much rarer because is was so difficult to make. The old time bowyers, both in this country and in Asia, added a belly to the bow which was able to withstand more compression. Horn was the most common material, either sheep or buffalo, although antler, such as elk or caribou, or even bone was used. These materials are brittle and it's amazing anyone ever thought to use them in a bow. Their brittleness, which makes them easy to break, is caused by their inability to withstand tension. On the belly of a bow, however, they only have to withstand compression, and accomplish this much better than wood.

The innovations were so effective the ancient Turks were able to shoot arrows over half a mile with their sinew-backed horn bows. Our modern bow technology, with all of its cams and cables and pulleys and fiberglass, cannot come close to equalling the distance of those "primitive" bows.

REGIONAL STYLES

Bows have been in North America for roughly five thousand years. During that time, a number of different types have evolved based on materials that were available, the climate, and the preferences of the bowyers. As a VERY general rule, hard woods, such as osage orange, were made into bows with a rectangular cross-section, while softer woods, such as yew, were used to make wider, thinner bows.

On the West Coast, the bow wood of choice was yew, although juniper as well as hickory and ash were used. This wood was made into wide, flat bows, usually with a narrowed handle. These bows were 1¼" to 1½" wide at the handle, 1¾" to 2⅛" wide at midlimb, and tapered to about 3/4" wide at the tips. Some of these bows were flat on the belly and slightly rounded on the back. Others were flatly eliptical in cross-section with the sinew backing coming all the way to the edges on each side. The Western Indians also made bows without the narrowed handle, these being 1¾" wide at the grip and tapering to 5/8" at the tips. The Western bows ranged in length from 36" to 56", but most were between 36" and 45". Almost every Western bow I have seen is sinew-backed, though usually with a very thin layer. Yew is so soft that even this thin layer of sinew gave the bows a reflex. The Western Indian bowyers did beautiful, painstaking work and produced excellent equipment. Perhaps their bows and arrows had to be well made and accurate because they stalked their game and usually managed just one shot.

In the Rocky Mountains and Great Basin the bows were constructed from ash, yew brought from the west, and some marginally effective bow woods like mountain mahogany and chokecherry. Due to the shortage of good bow woods they also made exquisite composite bows of sheephorn and buffalo horn which we'll discuss later.

A longer bow was used by Northeastern Indians, since they seldom backed their bows and hunted and fought on foot. Sadly, there are not many surviv-

Mojaves from the Western desert. Note blunt arrows for small game. Courtesy National Anthropological Archives.

Indian man
painted by
John White,
ca. 1585,
on the coast
of North Carolina.
Courtesy National
Anthropological
Archives.

ing examples of Eastern bows, since the Indians of that area were either pushed west or nearly killed off at a very early date. Another problem was, as O.T. Mason wrote in 1893, that;

> "The Iroquois tribes were among the first to receive firearms from the early settlers. On this account they soon abandoned the bow and the arrow. Colden says that they had entirely laid them aside in his day (1727)." [1]

The few Northeastern bows that I have examined or seen references to were 55-65" long, 1½"-1⅞" at the widest part, and sometimes narrowed at the handle. They were rectangular in cross-section. The Eastern tribes used ash, hickory, or locust for the most part.

The Southeastern Indians, such as the Cherokees, made bows with straight sides, with the widest part at the handle. They used primarily locust for their bows but sometimes used hickory and ash. In the western part of the south-

---

1. Mason, North American Bows, Arrows, and Quivers (1893, p. 649)

Chippewa hunters in birchbark canoe. Courtesy National Anthropological Archives.

east they would also use osage orange if they could get it. The bows ranged from 42" to 70" in length and were about 1¼" wide at the handle. Locust bows made by the Cherokees were laid out so the back half was sapwood and the belly half was heartwood.

In the central part of the country, around the headwaters of the Mississippi River, a flat, rectangular self bow was made. These bows were mostly made of ash or black locust, although a few were made of osage orange that was imported from further south. The Indians of this area, the Potawatomi, Sac and Fox, and Chippewa, normally made a simple bow about 50" long, but sometimes added a most unique feature. The entire right side of the bow was scalloped, giving a saw-tooth effect, and the edges of the scallops were painted. Sometimes both sides of a bow were treated in this way.

The people of the Missouri River drainage, such as the Pawnees, Osages, and Poncas, used osage orange for the most part, but occasionally used hickory. Osage orange is, in fact, named for the Osage Indians, who lived within its natural range. The Osage people lived on the border of the plains, and mostly used a rectangular, straight-sided self bow typical of the Plains Indians. However, they did make a few bows with a narrowed handle, more like an Eastern bow.

The Pawnee bows that I have examined were fairly short, about 45" to 50" long, made from osage orange, and unusually thick, powerful weapons,

WEST COAST
YEW, JUNIPER, ASH

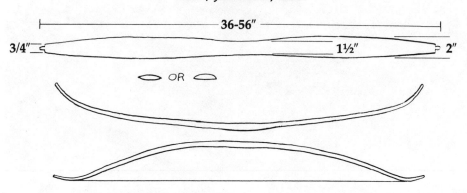

GREAT BASIN AND PLATEAU
BIGHORN SHEEP, BUFFALO, OR ELK HORN

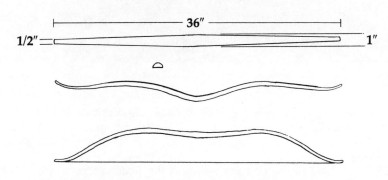

NORTHERN PLAINS
ASH

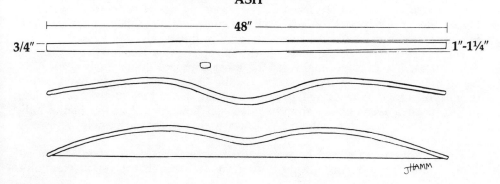

LOWER MISSOURI RIVER
OSAGE ORANGE

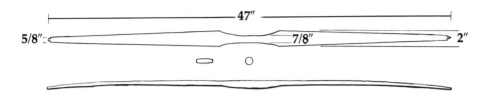

UPPER MIDWEST
ASH, BLACK LOCUST

CHIPPEWA

POTAWATOMI

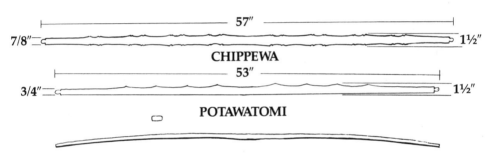

EAST COAST
HICKORY, ASH, BLACK OR YELLOW LOCUST

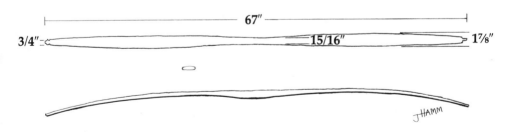

Every Native American group made the typical straight-sided self bow, but shown are some interesting alternatives. The bows on the left are sinew-backed and the ones on the right are self bows.

pulling 70 pounds or more. All Pawnee bows were almost certainly not this strong, but the ones I have seen indicate that the Pawnees were Olympic weightlifters.

In the Plains area horsemen prevailed, and their bows were normally shorter than those used by Indians who hunted on foot (with the exception of the sinew-backed yew bows). The Plains bows were usually 50", or shorter, and the handy, maneuverable weapons were ideally developed for horseback hunting or warfare. Rectangular in cross section, with the widest part of the bow being at the handle, most bows were 1" to 1¼" wide at the handle and about 3/4" wide at the tips. In pre-Columbian, pre-horse days the Plains bows were longer, about 55-60", and comparable to bows used by historical foot Indians.

To the Eastern Indians, single-shot muzzleloading firearms proved superior to bows because they were more accurate with greater range. On the wide-open Plains, however, where travel and fighting were usually done from horseback, the white frontiersman suffered a distinct disadvantage with their single shot weapons, since a muzzleloader was virtually impossible to reload from the back of a running horse. Any time white settlers were caught in the open and could not get to cover, they delivered one shot apiece and then were generally cut to pieces by the rapid-fire arrows. In fact, until the introduction of the repeating Walker revolver by Samuel Colt in 1839, the Plains Indians were much better armed for mobile combat than the white frontiersmen. The revolvers, and later the repeating Spencer and Henry rifles from the Civil War, finally swung the tide of firepower away from the Indians.

In modern times, Plains archery equipment has developed a poor reputation. Longbow shooters, and more recently, compound shooters tend to look askance at the short, and to their mind rustic, bows and arrows. Their prejudice against the horse Indians' weapons was not shared by anyone from the old days who faced them in a fight. "Bigfoot" Wallace, an early Texas Ranger, knew as much about Plains Indians as any white man of the last century. When Wallace heard a newcomer make a disparaging remark about the Indians' weapons, compared to the romance of English longbows, he replied:

> "I have seen a great many men in my time spitted with 'dogwood switches,' but I have never heard one of them yet complain of feeling anyways romantic under the circumstances. But the truth is, if you only understood the use of them, you might have a worse weapon than a good bow and arrows; at least, I know they are pretty dangerous in the hands of an Indian. They can shoot their arrows faster than you can fire a revolver, and almost with the accuracy of a rifle at the distance of fifty or sixty yards, and with such force that I have frequently seen them drive a shaft through and through a fullgrown buffalo" [2]

Wallace respected the Comanche and Kiowa bows and arrows much more than he did their ragtag collection of firearms. The Plains bows were not used in stand-up, long distance archery tournaments, but rather from the back of a running horse. It was this combination of horse and bow that helped make the Plains Indians so formidable in warfare.

2. Duval, The Adventures of Bigfoot Wallace (1966, p. 156)

Mounted Comanche man with bow & arrows. Author's collection.

The Northern Plains Indians principally used ash for their bows. The Sioux used hickory and chokecherry, as well. The Blackfeet utilized ash and hickory but obtained at least some osage orange through trade. Some Blackfoot bows (Museum of the Plains Indian, Browning, Montana) are made from osage orange with a sinew-backing, even though they were nearly a thousand miles from its natural range.

However, not everyone on the Central and Northern Plains had access to osage orange, as a pitched battle between the Cheyennes and the Kiowas during the 1830's illustrates. One of the principal men of the Kiowas was killed during a reckless charge among his enemies. His bow and other weapons were captured by the Cheyennes, but the Northern Indians did not recognize the bright yellow color of the osage orange, having never before seen it used for a bow [3].

Though not universal, the better northern bows were sinew-backed. Sioux bows were typically rectangular in cross-section, with the edges only slightly rounded. The sinew-backing did not come down over the edges, but was confined to the back. The bow had sinew wrapped around it every few inches to help prevent the backing from coming loose. In the North they also made composite bows from the horns of bighorn sheep, elk and buffalo, and occasionally from the bone of buffalo ribs. More on this in the section on composite bows.

On the Southern Plains osage orange was the overwhelming favorite for making bows. I've examined several dozen old Comanche and Kiowa bows belonging to museums and Indian families and every single one was made from osage orange. It was such a good bow wood that the Southern Plains Indians, to my knowledge, never had to sinew-back their bows, although some early travelers in the South vaguely refered to bows 'wrapped' with sinew. Since the Southern Plains bows were not backed, they were sometimes made longer than normally suspected for a horseback bow, up to 55″ or 56″. Most Southern Plains bows were 45″ to 50″, but these longer bows were not uncommon. The Comanches and Kiowas also, many times, left a layer of sapwood on their osage orange bows, while most other tribes typically removed it.

SELECTING, CUTTING, AND CURING WOOD

The two prime bow woods in North America are yew and osage orange, also known as bois d'arc, hedge apple, or horse apple. These two woods have the elasticity and speed of recovery that are necessary for an excellent bow. Speed of recovery refers to how fast the wood snaps back to shape when an arrow is released. A light bow with a quick recovery will often shoot an arrow faster than a heavier, more sluggish bow.

For osage orange and yew to be such exceptional bow woods they are almost opposites in workability and physical characteristics. Osage orange is extremely hard while yew is so soft it can be dented with a fingernail. Yew possesses a very fine grain, or yearly growth rings, while osage orange normally does not. A self bow made from yew should have a layer of sapwood left on the back of the bow to take the tension, while with osage orange it is not necessary. Yew, an evergreen, grows only on the higher elevations of the West Coast while osage orange is native to the Red River drainage of Oklahoma, Texas, Arkansas, and Missouri. Osage orange now grows throughout the Midwest as shelterbelts, planted for windbreaks, or as ornamentals. Either of these woods will make a fine bow with or without a sinew backing.

There are some other woods that I've made serviceable bows from although they're not as desirable as osage orange or yew. Ash makes a nice bow, especially when sinew-backed. Although hickory is durable, and easy to find in straight pieces, it is noticably slower than the prime bow woods and follows the string badly without a sinew backing. Another acceptable wood is black locust (not the honey locust we have here in Texas), which will make a useful

---

3. Powell, *People of the Sacred Mountain* (1975, p. 27-29)

Osage orange, left, and yew wood, showing the light colored sapwood and the dark heartwood. This also illustrates the relative size of the yearly growth rings.

bow with or without sinew. The yellow locust from the Southeast also makes a good bow. From the same family as osage orange, mulberry looks similar, though it's a pale yellow where osage orange is a bright, electric yellow. After yew and osage orange, I would classify mulberry, ash, and black and yellow locust as about even, followed by hickory.

We'll address the cutting of osage orange logs, although the methods remain the same no matter which wood is used. Try to cut the wood in winter for a couple of reasons. Not as much brush grows in the winter, which makes it easier to see a straight piece. Also, not as much sap is in the tree so the ends won't crack as badly during the drying period. Wood can be cut in the summer, but there will be quite a bit more waste due to splitting.

With any type of wood, look for a straight piece free from knots, cracks, and side branches. Cut as big a log as can be handled since the larger trees are normally cleaner (have grown around any flaws) and have straighter grain. With osage orange cut 10″ or bigger trees and take a 24″ tree if available. Osage orange smaller than 10″ may be straight but normally will be full of small knots where thorns and little branches grew. These smaller diameter pieces can be used but it's much more difficult to follow a single growth ring, which we'll get to later. If these smaller branches and trunks are all you have to work with, then by all means use them, but be prepared for some flaws. If you learn to make bows from the snarly, twisted, and knotfilled 3″ and 4″

End section of an osage orange log showing radial cracks caused by rapid drying.

branches, as I did, then it will seem like Christmas when you finally obtain a straight, clean stave. Your life will be simpler, however, if you cut as large a tree as you can handle at the start.

Always take as much straight wood as possible from a trunk. In other words, if there is 64" of good straight wood don't cut the trunk off at 48" because you only want a 48" bow. The extra wood will allow you to work around any flaws or cracks in the ends. And besides, you may change your mind and want a 64" bow, too. Be sure that the tree does not have a twist in it, you can usually tell if the bark seems to spiral around the tree even if the trunk is straight. A bow made from a tree like this will closely resemble a propeller.

After you've got a log cut and have it home, it's worthwhile to coat the ends of the wood to slow drying and help prevent cracking. Bowyers have used everything from lacquer to tar for coating the wood but I've come to prefer carpenter's glue for this task. The glue is relatively inexpensive, easy to apply, and thick enough to completely protect the ends. The glue does not completely stop the water from evaporating out of the ends, but greatly slows it down, limiting the drying cracks that would otherwise develop.

The whole log should be stored in the shade, off the ground, and out of the rain until you are ready to split it. The log can split immediately or stored in-

*Bow wood.
L. to R., 6" log,
2" limb, split
stave about 4"
wide, and four
staves cut with
a bandsaw.
These are all
resting on 15"
to 20" osage
orange logs.*

definitely but I usually like to reduce it within a couple of months of its being cut. The log is split lengthways into halves and then quarters with wedges, hammers, and axes. A good, straight piece of osage orange will split fairly easily, but if it's snarly and twisted be ready to work yourself to death. Be careful when hammering on the wedges because springy bow wood is bad about spitting them out. You can always tell old bowyers because they don't have any teeth.

Continue splitting the log lengthways into eighths or even further if it's big enough. It should be split into about 2" or 3" wide pieces. If you have access to a BIG bandsaw you can cut the quarter logs with it and get 1½" by 1½" staves and not waste any wood, however, few people have access to a twenty inch saw that can handle osage orange. Also, if you're just beginning, the wider split pieces give more room to work around a knot or crack.

In any case, once the log is split, the wood should immediately be reduced to stave size. Green wood will sometimes shrink and bends backwards, if it does this as a stave it gives you a built-in reflex. But, if it warps as a quarter log, all of the wood will be wasted except the strip right down the center, as the wood on either side of center will be unusable because it's bowed sideways instead of backward. This sounds a bit confusing, but the first time you split a log you'll see what I mean.

Once the log is split or sawed down to stave-size the bark should be removed. This will help prevent a nasty little creature known as the wood borer from invading your wood. The borer doesn't normally inflict much real damage, since he usually eats only the sapwood (I guess the hard heartwood dulls his teeth). Once in a while, though, he will eat down into the heartwood. A pile of sawdust under your hard-earned stack of staves will probably cause respiratory failure, but you shouldn't be too concerned.

After the bark is removed, dip the ends of the staves into the carpenter's glue to a depth of about two inches. Stack the wood flat, out of the weather, and in the shade to begin seasoning. There is a resin in osage orange, and other woods, that has to dry out and harden before the wood can be used for a bow.

For a self bow with no backing, osage orange needs to be dried at least two years. The longbow makers of the 1930's and 40's maintained it should be cured at least three years or longer. A good piece of osage orange that has been air dried for fifteen or twenty years was, and is, at a premium. On the other hand, a Comanche friend of mine makes his unbacked bows out of green osage orange, while it's still easy to work, and then oils them liberally. He makes some of the finest bows I've ever seen, but after six months or so must retiller them as the wood cures and gets stronger. As usual, there are two opposing ways to do the same thing, you can cure the wood for two weeks or fifteen years, but I think you'll find the two year seasoning period to be about right for unbacked osage orange bows.

If you plan to back your bow with sinew, osage orange can be used after a year of drying. The bow may get slightly stronger with age, as the sinew shrinks and the wood seasons completely, but the bow can always be lightened by scraping wood from the belly side.

With yew, the longbow makers of Great Britain aged a stave for seven years. Old-time bowyers in this country maintained that a four year seasoning was adequate. For an unbacked bow, I'd recommend at least a two year drying time. If you plan to back your yew bow the wood can be used after a year.

The other bow woods that have been mentioned should be seasoned for a comparable length of time, depending on the type of bow that will be made. The longer the wood can be seasoned, the better; however, I'm reasonably sure you want to make a bow while you're still young enough to pull it, so these shorter seasoning times should be sufficient.

Please keep in mind that these drying times don't begin when the tree is cut but rather when the wood is processed into staves. Also, if someone tries to convince you to use kiln dried wood for a bow, you should wave your arms and make horrible faces. If that doesn't scare him off, be prepared to run for your life. Kiln dried wood is brittle and will NOT make a bow, contrary to the advice that an "expert" gave me years ago, advice that was responsible for many of my early bow failures.

With so much trouble and curing time involved, you begin to see why bowyers develop into such wood mongers, always on the lookout for more good wood and reluctant to part with even the most pitiful stave.

SELF BOWS

A self bow does not describe who it belongs to but rather that the bow has been made from a single piece of wood.

You may want to exactly duplicate a particular type of Indian bow. If you wish to use this bow for hunting you'll want it to fit you and be as accurate as possible. In that case, keep in mind that the Indian men who made the museum pieces were shorter, on average, than we are today, so exact replicas of their equipment will be too small. You can make the same style bow they made, and make it from the same materials, but tailor the length to fit you.

If you are making the bow strictly for hunting, and are not interested in duplicating a particular tribal style, then a bow with a narrowed handle will probably be the best choice. The narrower handle allows the arrow to recover to a straight flight quicker, since it does not have to go around as much wood. A bow like this is more "center shot," and will generally be more accurate and easier to shoot.

Before we get into the actual construction of a bow, you need to figure out how long it will be. To accomplish that, first decide how long an arrow you

Cross-section of log showing orientation of bow.

want to shoot. For an unbacked bow, a good rule of thumb is to double the length of your arrow, then add ten to twenty percent to come up with the proper bow length. A sinew-backed bow is figured to be twice as long as the arrow it will shoot.

WORKING THE BACK OF THE BOW

The part of the stave that was towards the outside of the tree will be the back of the bow. The first step in turning a stave into a bow is to take the back down to a single growth ring. I cannot overemphasize this procedure, as it's crucial to the bow's durability. There's an old saying among bowyers that a bow at full draw is nine-tenths broken, but if you cut through the growth rings on an unbacked bow it will be completely broken, maybe not sooner but certainly later.

When a bow breaks, and I write this from sad personal experience, it almost always breaks from the back, the side of the bow that is under tension. Any crack, or knot, or place where the grain has been cut through becomes a place for the wood to start pulling apart. A sinew backing will overcome a multitude of problems and mistakes, but for an unbacked bow I always use the best piece of wood I can cut, beg, or borrow since the less flaws there are the less places it has to start breaking.

The growth rings to which I've been referring come from one year's growth of wood. The old-time bowyers tell me that seven to ten growth rings per inch is optimum, though I've made good bows with as few as four per inch to as

An osage orange log with ideal growth rings, about 7 to 10 per inch.

Working the back of the bow down to one growth ring with a drawknife.

many as thirty per inch. A small tree or branch tends to have fine growth rings, which are hard to follow. This is another good reason to cut a bigger tree if you can.

With osage orange the thick summer rings are hard and separated from each other by softer, flakier early spring growth. With the stave in a benchtop vise, cut down through the white sapwood with a drawknife until you reach the yellow heartwood. The drawknife should not be razor sharp, as it would have a tendency to dig into the wood. It may be hard to differentiate between layers in the sapwood, but once the heartwood is reached, the rings, and the flaky layers between them, should be distinctive. Start on one end and cut down into the heartwood for two or three growth rings. By looking at the end of the stave it is easy to see which rings are thick and which are thin. You'll want to get into a fairly thick ring for the back, especially if you're a beginning bowyer, since the thicker grains are easier to follow.

Once you've established which ring will be the back, work with the drawknife towards the other end of the stave. You may want to take off all of the

The back of the bow as it appears while being worked. The single growth ring has been established on the right side of the stave.

Same photo with edges of yearly growth rings outlined for clarity. The wood to the left is the highest, so this is where wood should be removed to get down to the established layer.

sapwood first, so you won't have to remove as much wood at one time. This is work, since osage orange is tough stuff. You'll quickly see the harder and softer layers of wood that I'm referring to in the heartwood, and with a little practice will be able to maintain a single layer throughout the length of the stave. When you're through, the back of the bow will be smooth, although probably not flat. Be sure to faithfully follow any dips or bumps or curves in the layer you are working, we'll take care of them later. Remember, a perfectly regular, straight, flawless piece of bow wood does not exist.

Having taken the stave down to one growth ring, there may be some flaws or imperfections that you can correct. Damage from wood borers or surface cracks can sometimes be eliminated by taking the back down another growth ring or two. Once the back is established this is not difficult, but make sure the stave will still be thick enough to accommodate your bow. Hazards like knots and deep end cracks cannot be solved in this manner since they go completely through the wood.

Now for the problem of knots. They're one of the most common problems with a stave, and since you often can't avoid them there's a way to live with them. With osage orange, you should be able to detect a knot as you go through the sapwood and into the heartwood. Work down to a single ring on one end of the stave as discussed earlier. When you get close to a knot, within 4-6 inches, you'll use the drawknife to "raise the knot." The annual growth rings will be raised up and distorted around a knot so this procedure leaves extra layers of wood around the flaw. Great care should be taken not to cut directly though a knot with the drawknife. If you cut through a knot, you would be cutting through the distorted layers of growth rings and creating a place for the bow to start breaking. Simply put the edge of the drawknife blade on top of the knot and begin carefully cutting wood away in all directions, until you've cut down to the established growth ring that was being worked. The extra layers of wood you are leaving will be above the growth ring you're working for the back of the bow, so this procedure will leave a bump, or wart,

Osage orange staves cut through with a saw to show the distortion around a knot. If the drawknife slices through one of these knots, the integrity of the bow's back will be lost.

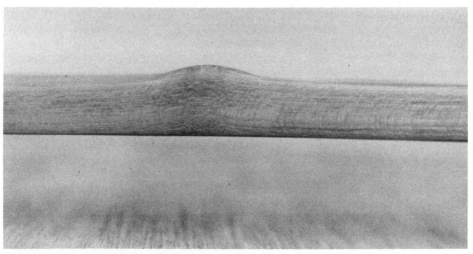

Edge of finished bow with raised knot.

around the knot with the knot itself being the highest part. The raised area should be a little smaller than the diameter of a dime and 1/16″ to 3/16″ tall. Be careful, also, to remain true to the growth ring that's being worked for the back, when leaving the extra wood for the raised area it's not difficult to lose track of which ring you're working.

Another strategy for dealing with knots in osage orange staves is to leave on a thin layer of sapwood about 1/16″ thick. Raise the knots as you normally would with heartwood. There are growth rings in the sapwood, too, so be sure to stay in the same one. If you aren't going to back your bow, any knots have to be handled with near perfection if they can't be avoided. You can understand why I save my very best knot free staves for unbacked self bows.

When making a self bow from yew wood, leave a thin (1/16″) layer of white sapwood on the bow as a backing. I prefer to lay out the bow, as described in the next section, and cut it out completely before removing any sapwood. With this method, you can look at the sides of the bow and tell exactly how much sapwood is left on, something that is difficult to do if a stave is 3″ wide and rounded. If you plan to back a yew wood bow, take off all of the sapwood down to the tan heartwood. In fact, following the grain with yew doesn't seem to be nearly as critical as with other woods if you're going to back it, which is a good thing, since yew is so close-grained and soft it is nearly impossible to stay within the same ring.

If you have one really good stave and four marginal ones, I strongly suggest you first try making bows with the rougher pieces. With what you learn from the first four, making a bow from the good stave should be no problem. However, if you start with the best piece and make a fatal mistake, which is not unlikely on a first try, your best wood will be gone when you figure out what you were doing wrong. Again, I write from bitter experience, and shudder to think about all of the good wood I've butchered over the years when first trying out a new idea or technique.

LAYING OUT THE BOW

We've already discussed the individual styles of bows and the different types of wood that can be used. Also, we've determined the bow length by doubling the arrow length and adding ten to twenty percent. With the bow style and length decided upon, we'll lay out its shape on the back of a stave that has been worked down to a single growth ring.

You will need a straight edge, such as a long ruler or length of lumber, as long as the bow you want to make. Lay the straight edge on the wood and visualize how the bow will be shaped. Here is where some extra wood on the ends and sides becomes helpful because you can often move the placement of the bow to avoid cracks or knots.

If a flaw is unavoidable, here are some tips to help minimize its effect. A knot becomes less dangerous if its location is an area of the bow that is not subjected to as much tension. The handle of a bow is normally left thick enough so that it doesn't bend much, if you can't steer clear of a knot try to place it in the handle. The last six inches or so on the tips of a bow can usually accommodate a knot, if it has been carefully worked. If you have a choice, place a knot in the center of a limb, rather than on the edges. A small crack on the end of a bow is normally tolerable, as long as it's not too large, and the crack remains within the bow and doesn't run out of the side.

It could be that you'll encounter a large knot with a rotten, punky center. Rather than give up on an otherwise good piece of wood, you can put in what is known as a "Dutchman's plug." This wasn't done on traditional bows but is a useful trick, nonetheless. With an unbacked bow you'll only want to attempt this in the handle section, but with a sinew-backed bow it will work anywhere except right on the edge of a limb. Raise the knot as you normally would, then drill out the rotten portion of the knot. Carve a plug from the same wood as your bow that just fits into the hole. Secure the plug flush with the back of the bow using carpenters' glue or hide glue. This technique can also be used successfully on unavoidable worm holes.

The flaws and problems you'll have to deal with are frustrating sometimes, but will improve your bowmaking abilities far beyond what would be possible if you had only perfect wood. As your skill and confidence increases you'll be able to make excellent bows from wood that was out of the question when you first began. Besides, the flaws you encounter and overcome will make good war stories and lies for other bowyers. You'll need these stories for self-defense, since bowmakers are among the world's worst liars (present company excluded, of course).

Anyway, once you have determined where the bow will go, find the centerpoint (half the length of the bow) and make a pencil line across the stave. Mark the ends, as well, if the bow doesn't go to the end of the wood. Lay the straight edge on the wood, where the center of the bow will be, and make a mark down its length.

I like to use a 5" handle on short bows and a 6" handle on longer ones. From the centerpoint of the bow, measure half the length of your handle in each direction and mark a line across the stave. At each of these lines, measure out from the centerline half the width of your bow at the handle and make a mark. Connect these marks and you should have a rectangular handle laid out

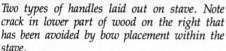

Two types of handles laid out on stave. Note crack in lower part of wood on the right that has been avoided by bow placement within the stave.

Same two bows completely laid out.

in the exact center of your bow. Now, at the tips, measure out half the width of the bow on each side of the centerline and make a mark. Connect this mark to the corner of the handle on the same side and the outside dimensions of your bow should be laid out.

Now, there are a couple of options. You can cut the bow out on a bandsaw and save a couple of hours work. Or, with a handaxe, you can CAREFULLY chop away the excess wood until you get down close to the pencil marks. You must be careful that the grain of the wood doesn't guide the axe into the area of your bow. When you see the grain starting to go into the bow, you can turn the stave over and remove wood from the other direction. The judicious use of a handaxe will save a lot of time, and is the method I use, but you must be careful not to ruin the stave. Another option is to rasp down to the marks while the wood is held in a vise. You'll have to work down to the pencil lines with a rasp even if you've bandsawed the stave or worked it with an axe, but on a particularly difficult piece of wood, to be safe, you may have to rasp away

Ishi, the stone-age Indian who walked out of the California wilderness in 1911, works a juniper stave with a handax ca. 1914. Courtesy Lowie Museum of Anthropology, University of California at Berkeley.

The author works an osage orange stave with a handax. The technology hasn't changed much.

all of the excess wood. This will be time-consuming and laborious, but, if you'd wanted to take the easy way out, you would have bought a compound to begin with.

At this point, the outside shape of the bow should be completely cut out, and the edges rasped right down to the pencil lines. Now we lay out the thickness, or depth, of the bow.

Contrary to what you may have seen or read, it is impossible to give exact thickness measurements in order to make a particular strength bow. Since every piece of wood is different, both in characteristics and curing times, I can only give you some starting dimensions for the bow and you can carefully take off wood from that point to get the weight you want. Since it would be very difficult to use a bandsaw or handaxe to take the belly of a bow down to the finished thickness, this has to be done slowly with a rasp or scraper. These are approximate FINISHED measurements, remember, you should start thicker than this (1/16" to 1/8" thicker) and slowly work the wood down towards this point as you test the weight of the bow.

Western Yew Bow : handle - 3/4", midlimb - 7/16", tip - 5/16"
Plains Bow : handle - 9/16", midlimb - 3/8", tip - 5/16"
Eastern Style Bow : handle - 1¼", midlimb - 9/16", tip 3/8"

Sighting down the edge of the bow to be sure wood is rasped off in a straight line.

Width of the bow is established and the depth laid out. Wood to the left of the line should be removed.

On each side of your stave, make a pencil mark at the handle, midlimb, and the tips for the appropriate thickness (the finished thickness plus the extra allowance). Connect these marks with a solid line. Wood can be removed down to this line in several ways. A bandsaw is the fastest, and this step doesn't take nearly as big a saw as cutting up logs. You can work down to the line with a handaxe, and if you work from the center out towards the tips, there is little danger of splitting the wood since you will be working out of the growth rings instead of into them. The stave can be put into a vise and the wood removed with a drawknife, but again, be sure to work from the center outward to avoid splitting the wood. Next, with a rasp, take off any leftover wood that is above the line. As you gain experience, you can work down closer to the finished thickness with a handaxe or drawknife to save some rasp work, but for now, the important thing is to make a bow rather than save time.

At this point, with the basic shape of the bow cut out, you can GENTLY bend the bow by holding a tip in each hand and putting a knee at the handle. Don't pull it much beyond where the bow will be when it's strung, you're only checking to see if one limb is harder to bend than the other. You're also checking to see if the entire bow is way too hard to bend, which it probably will be. You can take wood off with the rasp until the limbs pull more or less evenly and the bow is not pulling 140 pounds (refer to the later portion of this chapter on tillering). Be careful not to take off too much wood, if you want a 60 pound bow, at this stage it should still pull about 75 or 80 pounds.

BENDING AND SHAPING

A bow has to spring back to shape when an arrow is released, the faster this recovery takes place the faster a bow will shoot an arrow. One way to speed up this recovery is to bend the wood and "set back" the handle of a bow and "recurve" the tips. What this accomplishes, in effect, is to shorten the limbs of the bow and make the center part of the limb do more of the work. The working portion of the limb undergoes more compression and tension, which makes the bow shoot harder. It also makes the bow more prone to breakage since it's under more strain.

If you are making your first bow, you may want to forego the set back and recurves. Concentrate on making a shootable bow rather than the ultimate bow. However, even though this might be your first try, you may still have to do some bending since the limbs probably will not be the same and the bow may not be straight.

The bow wood, and especially osage orange, can be bent with heat. For an unbacked self bow, it is best if the wood is not heated and bent at all. If, as will probably be the case, it does require some bending, it should be done with steam or boiling water. This method does not dry out the wood and make it as brittle as direct heat. The part of the limb to be bent can be held over a kettle of boiling water until it becomes flexible, usually about thirty minutes. Another method is to have an iron pipe, 4" to 6" in diameter, with a threaded cap on one end. Fill the pipe about half full of water and prop the pipe in a firepit where it will not move. When a fire is built, and the water begins boiling, one end of the bow can be inserted into the pipe. Again, for self bows with no backing, use steam or boiling water if they must be straightened or if you want a setback or recurve.

For bows that will be sinew-backed, direct heat from a fire or electric range will work. I prefer a propane grill, the lid distributes heat evenly and the thermometer helps prevent the wood from becoming too hot. To help heat penetrate the wood, a thin coating of grease or shortening can be spread over the surfaces of the limbs. This also helps prevent scorching of the wood.

The bow, coated with grease, can be put into the grill one half at a time. Set the grill on low to medium. The wood needs to be turned occasionally as it heats, so it will get hot all the way through and won't scorch. Using potholders so as not to burn yourself, take the bow out and test it across your knee to see if the wood is ready to bend. Osage orange will reach a temperature where it becomes easy to bend, if it's still too stiff it needs to be hotter. Other bow woods can be bent in this way, yew in particular, but the others will not be as easy to bend as osage orange.

For a first bow, you'll probably just want to straighten out any kinks or bends in the wood until the bow is straight. Bend the flexible osage across a knee until the curve is gone and hold it there until it cools somewhat. Moderate kinks can be taken out in this way, although a severe wrinkle in the grain of the wood can't be heated enough to bend without scorching the wood. A sharp kink won't hurt the function of the bow, though the unkinked limb should be heated and bent until it has roughly the same shape. This will make tillering the bow easier.

Putting a set-back in a bow handle with heat. Note potholders to avoid burning hands.

A bow may have a side to side bend in it. If looking down the back of the bow, the limbs don't line up or one limb is cocked off to one side, it can be straightened during the heating process. Bend the hot wood to take out the crookedness, and go a little past straight with it. A bench-top vise and wooden chucks are handy for this. So are the upright forks of a tree; place the heated crooked side of the bow between the branches and pull on the other end. But be aware, with either of these methods, that the wood can't tolerate too much sideways bending.

The wood might also have a propeller twist in it, where one tip is turned in relation to the other. The bow can be heated, placed in a vise, and one tip turned with a wrench until the tips line up. Pad the jaws of the wrench so as not to mar the wood. A severe twist like this might be difficult to take out, and the wood may have to be reheated several times. Whenever one limb is

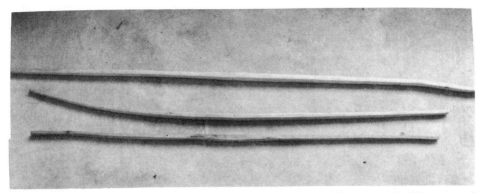

Bows showing original shape. A single growth ring was faithfully followed and the dimensions of the bow are cut out.

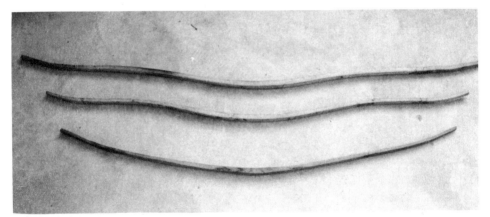

Shape of bows after heating and bending.

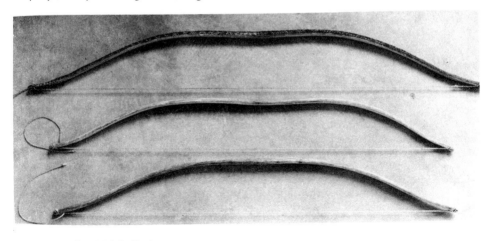

Same bows after initial tillering.

heated to solve a problem, be sure to heat the other limb too, either with steam or direct heat, whether it needs to be bent or not. This equal treatment keeps both limbs even and gives them the same stiffness.

To put in a set back at the handle the bow needs first to be straightened. Then heat the center of the bow and bend it backwards over a knee using the potholders to protect your hands. The middle portion of a bow, being thicker, will have to be heated more than the thinner tips. If the handle is too thick, you may not be able to get it hot enough to bend without scorching (a spliced bow, a modern innovation made out of two pieces of wood joined at the handle, is used to give a set back to a thick handled bow). The heated wood can take a considerable set back, but can only stand a certain amount of this backwards bending; watch the belly to make sure the wood is not splitting. A wooden jig can also be used for this step, with clamps to hold down the heated wood. Again, try not to bend the wood so far that splitting occurs on the belly side.

Graceful recurved tips will add much to the speed and symmetry of a bow. As before, bend the heated bow, in this case the tip, over the knee until the wood cools somewhat. When one tip is the proper shape, heat and bend the other. If necessary, reheat one or both in order to make them match exactly. Or, the heated tip can be placed in a padded vise and the bow pulled for leverage. This step can also be done with a jig, although I prefer to bend the wood by hand because there is better control. When heating the wood in this fashion, about a forty-five degree bend can be placed in the tip; any more than that, and there is a real danger of the wood splitting. The wood can be boiled for about an hour and put in a jig if you require more of a bend. For most purposes, however, the direct heat and grease work well if you plan to sinew-back the bow. Again, if you are not backing the bow, stick with steam or boiling water for any required bending.

If you choose to back the bow, refer at this point to the section on sinew-backing. If not, proceed to the nocks.

NOCKS

After shaping the bow, the nocks for a string must be cut so the process of stringing and tillering can begin.

The system of double nocks found on some Indian weapons is the easiest and quickest to use. It is especially effective when used with a string that has a loop plaited or tied into one end. The majority of Indian strings did not have the plaited loop, they normally used a slipknot arrangement. Many of the Plains bows had only a single nock on each end for a simple reason; a slipknot was easier to loosen and get out of a single nock than a double. Other bows, particularly horn bows, had only a ridge of sinew on each end for a nock, the slipknot would tighten down above the ridge and hold securely.

A reproduction museum piece should have the same kind of nocks as was on the original. You may, however, be making the bow strictly for shooting and hunting, not being especially concerned with original nocking styles. If your primary focus is on utility, then I would recommend using a double nock and making strings with a plaited loop in the upper end (see chapter on strings).

L. to R., West Coast-style nock, narrow double nock, wide double nock, single nock of the Plains, and sinew nocks on a horn bow.

The nocks can be cut in with a sharp knife, a round file, or even a Dremel tool. Smooth the edges carefully so they won't cut the string.

TILLERING

Tillering involves taking wood off of the belly of a bow until both limbs pull evenly. But it borders on art to reduce the draw strength of the bow to the desired weight while keeping both limbs evenly balanced. If a bow is reduced to the proper weight, but one limb is still stronger than the other, then more wood has to be taken from the stronger limb. Of course, this decreases the bow's strength from what was desired. If too much wood is taken from the stronger limb, the stronger limb is now the weakest and wood must be taken from the other limb to make them even again. This further reduces the bow's strength. Naturally, I've done this, and made a 40 pound bow from one that was intended to be 65 pounds. As mentioned, there is some art involved.

A self bow, with no backing, should have the back sanded perfectly smooth before the tillering process begins. The reason for this is that a bow will usually begin breaking at an imperfection, a knot, where the grain has been cut through, or at a dent or bump in the back. Engineering tests done on metal show that the metal almost always fails at a dent or scratch. The sanding will smooth the back of the bow and help remove any flaws. This may not be necessary and with added experience you may wish to forego this step, but at this point it is just added insurance against the bow's breaking. Be careful not to take off much wood during the sanding, especially refrain from going down through the established growth ring. Start with 220 grit sandpaper, go to 320, 440, and finally 600. If you use a vise, you'll want to pad the jaws to protect the sanded back from dents so it won't have to be sanded again later.

Stringing a bow by stepping through it. This method offers the most control if the bow is long enough to permit it.

Stringing a shorter bow by using the instep of one foot to support the lower limb. The right hand pushes down, while sliding the string, as the left hand pulls up on the handle.

The first step in the artistic tillering process is to work the bow down until it can be strung. If the bow is too powerful to be strung, wood should be rasped evenly from the belly side of both limbs. Bend the bow across the knee to feel the strength and also to make sure the limbs pull evenly. Be careful to control the bow; I once had a highly reflexed bow slip when pulling it across my knee. The bow reversed in my grip and broke at the handle.

Take off just enough wood so you can get the bow strung, at this point the bow should still be 10 or 15 pounds stronger than you want it. A word about how to adjust the string length on the bow. I personally like for the string to be tight enough so that when an arrow is put on the string, the feathers won't touch the bow. This means the string should be about 5-6" from the belly of the bow when it's strung.

Once the bow is strung, it will be easy to see if the limbs pull evenly. Place the bow on a square tile floor, or on a graph drawn on the wall, and any irregularities

Bending the bow to see if the limbs are even. Don't bend the bow any further than it will be bent when strung.

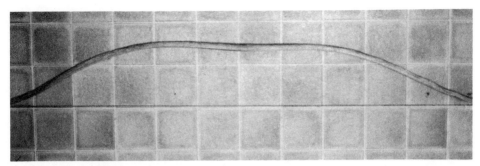

Once the bow is strung, a tile floor or a grid helps to show which limb is the strongest. Wood should be removed from the right limb of this bow as it's the stiffest.

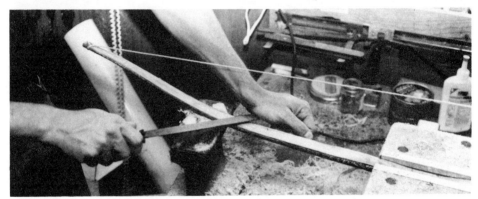

Rasping wood from the belly of the strung bow.

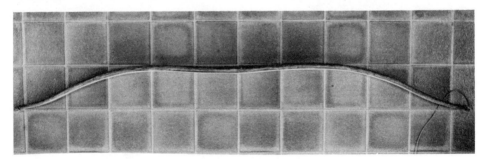

The bow now pulls fairly evenly and is ready to be drawn.

will be apparent. If one limb is stronger, or if there is a stiff place in one limb, the strung bow can be placed in a vise and wood carefully and slowly removed with a rasp. Be sure not to take off wood in just one spot, use long sweeping strokes with the rasp. If there is a sharp bend in the bow, then mark the spot with a pencil and remove wood from either side of the bend. The limbs should have an even, graceful bend. Proceed slowly, this is not a race.

Testing the weight of a bow. Note bottom end of stick resting on bathroom scale.

Pulling the bow to its full draw length as marked on the stick.

At full draw the weight of the bow will register on the scale.

When both limbs are roughly balanced, and have a graceful curve with no angular bends, you'll want to begin pulling the bow. Pull very gently at first,

20 or 30 times, and slowly increase the length of draw as you continue working the bow. Pull the bow back only about half way at this point. Again, place the bow on the graph and check for even, equal bending in the limbs. If the limbs remain balanced, you can continue drawing the bow, slowly increasing the pull until it is at full draw. If the bow is a great deal stronger than you want, it should not be brought to full draw until the weight is reduced. The stronger the bow, the more stress is put on the wood, so the more subject it is to breakage. Don't risk pulling the bow to full draw at 80 pounds if you only want a 55 pound bow.

If the limbs are still closely balanced, the time has come to check the weight of the bow. Place the bowstring in the groove on the weighing stick and place the stick on the bathroom scale as shown. Zero the scale. Pull the bow downward until you get close to your draw length, as marked in advance on the stick, and watch the scale. If you get close to the full draw length and the bow is still clearly too strong, and it should be if you've gone slowly to this point, more wood needs to be removed.

A tillering board with the bow placed on it, will help show up uneven areas in the limbs. Use this tillering board in conjunction with the square tile floor or wall graph. Take off wood very slowly when you get close to the finished weight. The belly can either be kept flat or slightly rounded from the center to the edges, it's up to the bowyer. The bow should always be drawn at least 20 or 30 times whenever wood is removed. Many times the bow has to be drawn before the effect of rasping wood from a limb becomes apparent. If enough wood is taken off to visually even up a stronger limb, when the bow is pulled that limb may give and be weaker than you thought. Again, take off wood very slowly and work the bow every time wood is removed.

When your bow, at long last, reaches the weight that you want and both limbs pull evenly, shoot a few arrows with the unfinished bow over a period

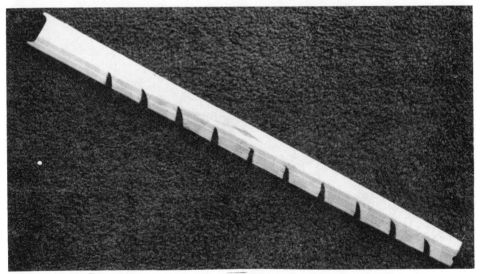

A tillering board. The handle of the bow goes into the groove on the left end of the board.

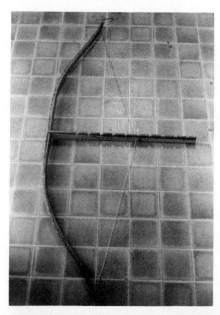

Using the tillering board in conjunction with a grid will help show where wood needs to be removed.

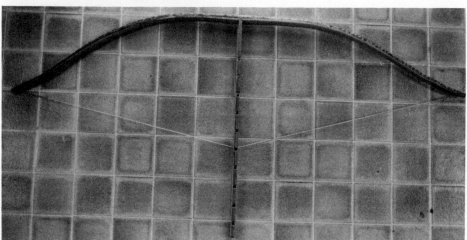

The right limb is slightly stiffer, and stronger, than the other and should have a very small amount of wood removed from the belly. It is time to go slowly, as this bow is close to being finished.

of several days. After this time, if the bow is still perfectly tillered, it is ready to finish. If not, it may need a little more wood taken off to even up the limbs. The bow may be at the exact weight that you want, and one limb may still be slightly stronger than the other. In this case, I would put the stronger limb on the bottom of the bow, since the bottom limb will usually be placed under slightly more strain when the bow is gripped at the center.

The bow may be lighter than you wanted because too much wood was taken off. The bow can be sinew-backed, which will add weight to it, but there is an easier way to make the bow stronger. You can cut an equal amount off of the tip at either end and cut new nocks. Recently, I had an unbacked osage orange bow that was 60" long and pulled 47 pounds at a 28" draw. I wanted it to be stronger and so cut 1" from each end and fashioned new nocks. The bow is now 58" long and pulls 53 pounds at the same 28" draw length. Since an equal amount was cut from both tips, the tiller of the bow didn't even change. Of course, making the bow shorter subjects it to more stress and increases the chance of breakage, but if the piece of wood is clean and any flaws or knots have been well worked, it's an effective, simple way to make a bow stronger. This method also will work with a sinew-backed bow, though I would want to wrap the tips with sinew for three or four inches before cutting the new nocks.

During the tillering process, when the bow is within 5 or 10 pounds of the finished weight, be sure that the limbs are properly lined up. Ideally, looking down the belly of a strung bow, from tip to tip, the string would lie exactly in the center of the bow. The string will sometimes be off to one side on one end. Many times this can be corrected by reheating the bow and bending the limb back into line (this is for a self bow only, not sinew-backed). At times this can be corrected by cutting the nock a bit deeper on the side the string slants off to. Another problem you may see is the string lying slightly off to one side of the bow, though the limbs are straight and the bow is evenly tillered. In this case, I will turn the bow so the string lies to the side the arrow will shoot across, to the left of the bow for right-handers and the opposite for left-handers. It is sometimes better to live with a problem like this than to risk creating a bigger problem by taking off more wood, or reheating and twisting on limbs that are almost exactly right anyway.

If your bow is the weight you want, the limbs are still even and well tillered after a couple of days of shooting, and the string is lined up to your satisfaction, then it's time to finish the bow and add a few aesthetic touches.

FINISHING

Upon reaching the finishing stage the bow will be slick on the back from working down to one grain with the drawknife and from sanding (you have been careful not to rasp or damage the back in any way, I hope). The sides and belly of the bow will be rough from the rasp marks.

The finishing process begins by scraping the belly of the bow to smooth out the marks from the rasp. Do this with a sharp blade (a pocket knife works fine) that is held at right angles to the wood. Place the bow in a vise and begin scraping from the center of the bow outward. Use long even strokes that take off a thin shaving at a time until the rasp marks are gone. If the blade starts to jump and make tiny ridges, scrape that section from the other direction or try changing the angle of the blade. This will normally occur around knots so you may have to scrape the knot area separately to get rid of the rasp marks. Broken glass or flint chips also work well for this scraping process.

Take off enough wood to get out the scratches, but no more. When the belly of the bow is smooth, check the tiller one last time. The tiny amounts of wood taken off in scraping should not change the tiller or the weight of the bow, but

Scraping out the rasp marks with a blade held at right angles to the wood.

I always check to make sure. If one limb is found to be slightly out of balance, the belly of the strung bow should be scraped. The scraper takes off very little wood, so this process is slow, but you want to go slowly and carefully at this stage.

When the belly is smooth, the sides need to be treated in the same fashion. The abrupt edges need to be scraped as well, although I only like to round them slightly. Once all of the rasp marks are gone, and the wood completely smooth, the bow can be sanded. Start with 220 grit, go to 320, then 400, and finish with 600. The entire bow should be sanded perfectly smooth. This will put a glossy surface on a hard wood such as osage orange but you can take the sanding one step further by burnishing. A smooth, rounded surface, such as a polished bone or even a small bottle, is used to rub the entire bow. This

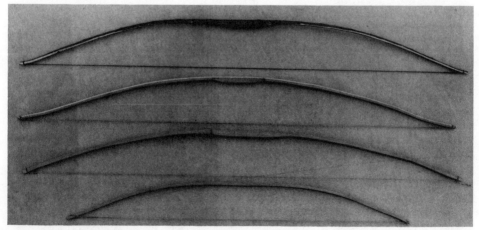

Finished self bows, all made from osage orange. The three on top are eastern style and the bottom one is a short plains bow.

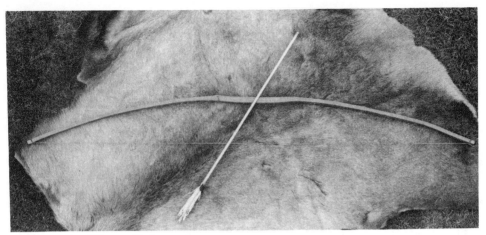

Osage orange self bow with dogwood arrow.

rubbing compresses and polishes the surface of the wood yielding a natural mirror-like finish.

Next, oil the bow to prevent its drying out and becoming brittle. Any light oil, or even shortening or bacon grease can be used. Bear grease or fat from a deer also works well if you can get it. Put the bow across both knees, then apply the oil or grease, and rub the wood with both hands from the center out to the tips, and back again. As you rub the oil into the wood, the bow will warm up due to friction. The front and back of the bow should be treated for ten minutes or longer. The wood becomes quite warm, if you rub vigorously, and this aids in the penetration of the oil. This hand-rubbed finish brings out the beauty of the wood and forms a barrier to protect the bow from moisture. The bow needs to be oiled regularly, at least every couple of months.

Now, unless you want to decorate or put a handle on the weapon (see chapter on decoration), the bow is finished. It can be admired as a work of art and as a deadly weapon, for it is both of these.

As you hold the beautiful finished weapon in your hand, the idea of actually wanting a compound bow seems pretty far-fetched, doesn't it?

SINEW-BACKED BOWS

First, the good news about sinew-backing a bow.

The sinew will cure almost any problem on the back of the bow, such as knots, cutting through the grain, or cracks. If unsure about the piece of wood you are working, then I suggest you sinew-back it.

As the sinew cures and dries after being applied to the back of the bow, it shrinks. This tightly stretched layer of sinew makes a bow shoot harder and faster. One of my sinew-backed osage orange bows, pulling only 53#, shot a 28" arrow through a chronograph at 180 feet per second. An impressive performance, considering that a commercial longbow drawing 70# shot the same arrow only 5 feet per second faster. The sinew also helps retain whatever shape you put into a bow with grease and heat. It prevents the bow from 'following the string.'

Sinew's ability to hold the back of a bow together and prevent it from breaking, will let you use a shorter bow to shoot an arrow. These short bows are pulled further, and therefore develop more compression and speed than an unbacked longer bow. With sinew you may be able to use a stave that would otherwise be too short, which is helpful, since good bow wood is so difficult to come by. The shorter bows are also handy in actual hunting situations. In a tree or in thick brush, the short bow is a natural. If you plan to carry or use a bow on horseback, the short bow becomes essential.

There is nothing to prevent backing a longer style bow if you wish. The sinew will render the bow almost unbreakable and add speed to its delivery. Sinew-backing is normally associated with bows that shoot arrows half their length, but its advantages can be united with an English-style longbow that is 72" long and shoots a 28" arrow.

To my mind, a sinew-backed osage orange or yew wood bow is the ultimate hunting weapon. They are light, extremely fast shooting, and useful in almost any hunting situation.

Now, for the bad news about sinew-backing a bow.

First of all, it's an awful lot of trouble. Backing a bow will at least double the amount of time necessary to make a bow.

Also, materials are sometimes hard to come by. Elk, deer, or buffalo sinew has to be saved in advance or ordered from afar. Hide glue, for applying the sinew, is time consuming to make, and very difficult to find commercially in quantities of less than a hundred pounds.

The sinew-backing is also affected by moisture. In very damp weather the bow will lose some of its speed, and if the bow is soaked long enough the backing can be ruined. There are measures to protect the backing from moisture, but with wet weather hunting this could be a consideration, depending on your climate and the intended use of the bow. Keep in mind that enough moisture to damage the bow will completely ruin handmade arrows, fletched with sinew and hide glue, so you probably won't be using the weapons in marginal weather anyway.

Another drawback to the shorter bows is that they are harder to shoot well. A short bow, be it fiberglass recurve, compound, or sinew-backed wood bow, can be mastered but it will take more practice since any shooting mistakes are amplified with the shorter limbs. A longbow is the most forgiving and the easiest to shoot, but the shorter bows are accurate out to 25 or 30 yards, which is acceptable for most types of hunting.

Some people complain about 'finger pinch' with the shorter bows. They claim that the severe angle the string makes when shooting is troublesome. Most people never notice it, though, since the angle is no different than that of shooting an arrow from a modern fiberglass recurve. If you are concerned about it, try shooting a recurve and see if it bothers you. If so, you can always make a longer bow in a style you like.

It may sound like a contradiction, but for a first bow it may be easier to sinew-back it. This is because the sinew, if applied correctly, will probably allow you to make a shootable bow on the first try. The forgiving qualities of sinew will cover up any problems or mistakes in a piece of wood. The sinew-backed bow may take twice as long to make, but the chances of it breaking are a fraction of that for an unbacked bow.

There you have it, the pros and cons of sinew. If you are undecided about which type of bow to make, I suggest you make one of each.

PREPARING THE STAVE

The stave for a sinew-backed bow should be handled exactly like a self bow up through the shaping of the wood, as described earlier. Once the stave has been roughed in and shaped with heat, it is nearly ready to sinew-back. I never pull a bow until the sinew is cured, so there is no need to cut nocks into the wood until later. Early in my bowmaking career, I felt that a bow should be tillered and tested before the sinew was applied. The theory being that if a bow was going to break, much better for it to break before I had gone to all the trouble of putting the sinew on. A lot of bows with knots and other problems did break. Only after destroying at least half a dozen good bows did it start to dawn on me that the sinew was what kept a bow from breaking, that a bow should never be pulled until the sinew was on it. I never claimed to be quick, just persistent.

The roughed-in bow, shaped with heat, can be GENTLY bent across your knee to see if one limb is greatly stronger than the other. Wood can be rasped from the belly of the stronger limb, as described in the tillering section. Keep in mind that at this point the bow should be a great deal stronger than the finished weight. Don't get too carried away with making the limbs match perfectly or in reducing the weight of the bow, just get them fairly close and we'll take care of it after the sinew is on.

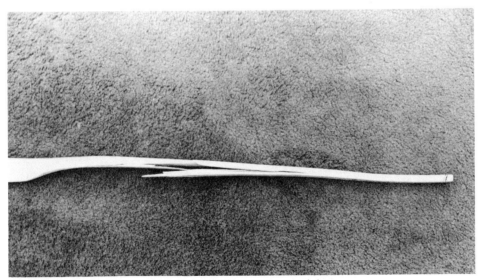

If you make enough bows sooner or later you'll get to see one of these.

PREPARING SINEW

The sinew from any large animal can be used to back a bow. Every animal, from a mouse to a musk ox, has sinew, but in order to obtain the lengths necessary for a bow, an animal from deer or antelope size, on up, is needed. Animals such as horse and cattle will work, although with the many hours necessary to make a bow, I prefer to use materials from the 'original' wild animals.

The most commonly available sinew comes from the deer. Many people hunt their own deer, or have friends that do, or you can go to a processing plant that does custom butchering during deer season. Modern butchering destroys the back sinew, but most plants cut off the legs at the knees and throw them in a barrel. This can be a year's supply of leg sinew if you don't mind some strange looks when asking for the legs. Some gracious butchers will even let you cut out the sinew on site, so later you don't have the problems of disposing of the leg bones and hooves. Sometimes you can obtain a couple of hundred sinews in a single afternoon.

Deer sinew works very well, as does elk. Although noticably stiffer and harder to work, elk has the advantage of being longer. Buffalo is about the same length as elk but is much easier to work because it's softer. It splits relatively easily and is the same thickness throughout its length. I've come to prefer working with buffalo sinew, although it is usually difficult to find. Elk tendon seems to impart a little more tension to the bow, but the difference is so small it may only be my imagination.

Sinew is found in two primary areas on an animal. The back, or loin, sinew is a thin sheet of tissue which is on top of the backstraps, the long piece of meat which lies down either side of the backbone. The sinew will appear white when the animal is being butchered, and a deer will usually yield a 10" to 15" piece. This back sinew will be about two inches wide and very thin. The fresh sinew should be placed flat on a smooth surface (I use the hood of my pickup), and any adhering meat scraped free with a knife blade held at right angles to the sinew. Leave the sinew stuck to the flat surface until dry, then peel it free and store it in a dry place, where it will keep indefinitely.

The other source of sinew comes from the legs of animals, from their Achilles tendon. This tendon lies down the back of each leg, in a groove in the bone, and a deer should yield at least a 10" piece if it is carefully removed past the knee joint. The sinew will be white and about as big around as your little finger. It should be laid out in the sun to dry, out of the reach of varmints (like my two Beagles, for instance). Once dry, the sinew will be hard and amber in color. It must be completely dry before you store it.

Either loin or leg sinew works well for backing a bow, but I've come to save the thin loin sinew for fletching arrows and attaching points. If you wish to use it for backing a bow, just split it down into narrow pieces and soak these in the hide glue. The back sinew has to be soaked much longer than leg sinew before it becomes limp enough to put on the bow, which is another reason I save loin sinew for fletching.

To prepare the dried leg sinews, they first have to be pounded. I use a hammer along with an anvil made from a section of railroad track, but beating the sinew with a rock works just as well. Be careful when pounding the sinew not

L. to R., elk leg tendon, pounded tendon with outer shell starting to loosen, tendon beginning to be reduced, single tendon pulled apart into eighths, reduced to final thread size.

to cut it by hitting it with the edge of a hammer or rock. Pound the sinew thoroughly; it will turn white and begin to flatten and separate. I usually work about a dozen sinews through this process at a time.

When the sinews are pounded, there is an outer covering on the tendon that will start to separate. This needs to be removed and two pairs of pliers are sometimes necessary to pull it loose. Discard this outer shell. The inner tendon, which is what you'll be using, can be pounded again to aid in the separation of the fibers. The tendon then has to be pulled apart. Most of the time, it can be split in half, but on a really tough one a smaller piece may have to be stripped away. Again, two pairs of pliers are useful when the tendon is first separated.

All of the tendons you're working should be pulled apart into eighths and put together in a pile. These pieces are then separated down to the small fibers that are needed to back a bow. The sinew should be reduced until it's about the size of a piece of string. Twelve to fifteen of these small fibers are placed into bundles. When reducing the sinew, I usually have about four or five different lengths of bundles being worked at the same time. When a bundle gets enough fibers in it, I place that bundle between the pages of a magazine, turn the page, and then start on another bundle of the same length. Placing each bundle between the pages of a magazine is a handy way to store them and helps keep them separated and intact. Try to keep the fibers about the same length when putting them into bundles, it will be easier to place them on the bow. Also, don't get caught up in only having long bundles of ten or twelve inches. You'll need these long ones for the body of the bow, but

A pounded tendon spread apart to show the interlocking fibers.

don't overlook the medium and short bundles which are necessary for the sides and ends.

Some of the sinew threads may require trimming with scissors if they are thick on one end. Occasionally one end of a portion of tendon will be stiff and no amount of pounding will soften it. It's better to cut the stiff area off and use what you can. Separating the sinew and evening it up by judicious trimming is time consuming and tedious. However, extra care taken during this step will result in a much neater finished product and will be worth the additional effort.

The ends trimmed off of the sinew, as well as the debris left over from stripping it out, may be saved to make your own hide glue if you wish. We'll discuss glue in the next section, but for now, save the clean, white sinew scraps, although you can discard the greasy outer covering of the tendons.

How much sinew to put on a bow? Even a very thin layer, or one complete course, will greatly enhance the durability of a bow. For added speed and strength, I like to put on at least four courses and sometimes up to six or seven. On an average bow, 50" to 55" long, it figures out to between 150 and 250 bundles, or about six elk leg tendons. On a longer bow it should take proportionately more. If you think it will take 250 bundles, it's better to have up to 300 ready. If there are any left over you can use them on the next bow or make bowstrings out of them. You'll also need some extra bundles to wrap the ends after the sinew is cured.

The sinew should be reduced to this size for backing a bow.

PREPARING GLUE

Glue for bonding the sinew to a bow is made from animal by-products like hide shavings and sinew scraps. No other glue, such as epoxy or other modern glues, will do the job. The 'hide glue' is compatible with the sinew since it is made from the same animal protein, and forms a solid matrix on the back of the bow. Modern glues are not needed anyway, since hide glue is incredibly strong if properly applied. I once tried to remove the sinew-backing from a bow. After peeling up the sinew at one tip, I was able to grasp the backing with a pair of vise grips. With the aid of a great deal of black language and a modest amount of sweat, the sinew finally came loose for about a foot. Imagine my surprise when I discovered that the sinew had not been pulled loose from the wood, but rather that the wood, in this case osage orange, had been split and a layer had come loose with the sinew-backing. If you've worked with osage orange, you'll be impressed, as I was, with a glue that is strong enough to destroy the wood rather than allow the backing to come loose.

There are two ways to get serviceable hide glue. The first is to make it yourself, and although it takes at least 24 hours, it can be a worthwhile project. The glue is made from fine hide shavings that come from a skin when it's scraped prior to being brain-tanned. These hide shavings are about like light, loose sawdust. The glue can also be made from sinew scraps that are left over after pounding up the tendons and separating them down to thread size. The hide shavings and sinew scraps can be combined in the same batch of glue with no detrimental effects.

The raw materials are placed in an old pan, then very warm, almost hot, water is added. After the mixture has simmered for awhile, you can skim off any dirty debris that comes to the surface. An alternative is to pour off the initial amount of water after fifteen minutes or so and replace it with fresh water. The water and animal products are then simmered for hours, with fresh water added occasionally to replace that lost from evaporation. After a day, and maybe two, depending on the relative humidity, properties of the hides, and the way you hold your mouth, the hide shavings will melt away. What is left is an amber colored glue. If you use sinew scraps they will shrivel up and have to be strained or picked from the glue.

If you don't want to go to the trouble of making your own hide glue, there is a commercial glue called powdered hide glue that is just as effective. Place it in the double boiler with warm water until the dry powder soaks up the liquid and reconstitutes. This glue is handier than making your own because it is ready to use in an hour. Powdered hide glue is rather difficult to find, though you might try an artists' supply or furniture manufacturer. There are different grades of it, too, with some setting up very quickly when you're applying sinew, while other grades don't set up for an hour. You'll want a grade about in the middle, one that will give you some time to work the sinew, about ten minutes.

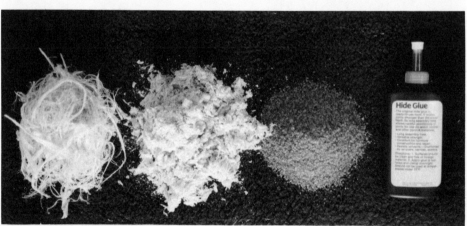

L. to R., sinew scraps, deer hide shavings, powdered hide glue, and liquid hide glue.

The thickness of hide glue is determined by two factors, water content and temperature. Once the glue is made, either from scratch or with powdered glue, you can use it at once while it is hot or let it cool and congeal. The congealed glue, which is about like thick Jello, can be stored for a week or so in the refrigerator before it starts to dry out. It only has to be reheated in order to be reconstituted, a process that can be done with the double boiler. It can also be done with the judicious use of a microwave, set on high for about 10 seconds at a time and then stirred, until the glue is warm and liquid (I can hear the purists gnashing their teeth in the background).

Glue that is liquid can be dried and stored, if you wish. This is especially useful if you make your own in a large batch and want to save it. Place the glue in a refrigerator until it congeals, then cut the glue into manageable pieces, maybe 2″ by 1″. They are left in the refrigerator for several days, until the glue starts to harden. The pieces are then threaded onto a length of string and hung up in a cool place to completely dry where they can't touch anything and stick to it. Once the pieces are dry they will be hard and can be stored indefinitely. When you get ready to reconstitute the chunks of glue, just place as many as you need in a bowl and cover them with warm water the night before you'll need them. The next day, you can put the glue in the double boiler to keep it warm. Add water as needed until the glue is the right consistency, about like thin syrup. When you're ready to apply sinew, the glue should be very warm to the touch, but not uncomfortably hot.

You may come across what's known as liquid hide glue, which comes in a plastic bottle. You'll probably be tempted to use it for applying sinew, since it's already a liquid and is very easy to use. Don't succumb to the temptation, as I did, for the liquid glue will cause a bow to break (I only had to break about three bows to figure this out, I was really proud of myself). This glue has a chemical additive, known as a retarder, which keeps the glue liquified and prevents it from setting up. It dries so slowly that the sinew will begin shrinking and pulling away from the bow where there is a recurve or setback in the wood. This all takes place next to the wood, and is very difficult to see, but

Double boiler (actually a liberated crock-pot) to keep the glue hot. Note stirring stick in water to prevent glue from sticking to it and insulated cup with warm water to add to glue.

the net effect is that the sinew does not touch the wood. This causes the bow to break, which is most undesirable.

The liquid glue is excellent, however, for fletching and putting points on arrows. The glue does not have to be 'made up,' and is simply squeezed from the bottle and can be used in very small quantities. You'll probably want to get some for arrowmaking. A hobby shop or hardware store may carry it, but I've always been able to find it at Sears, although not every Sears store has it.

PREPARING THE BOW

Glue and grease are not compatible, and the bow was greased when it was heated and bent. Grease and oil from your hands have also contaminated the wood as you handled it. In order for the glue to properly hold the sinew to the bow, the wood has to be carefully treated and degreased.

The first step in preparing the wood is to rasp the back of the bow to give the glue a rough surface to cling to. Don't take off much wood, just roughen the smooth surface left from when the stave was drawknifed down to the single growth ring. Be careful not to cut through the growth ring established for the back. At this stage you'll want to slightly round the edges and the ends of the bow with the rasp, as well.

Next, the surface of the wood has to be degreased. In the old days, wood ashes and water were used to make lye to cut the grease, but it is easier to use commercial lye crystals designed for clearing clogged drains. Some drain cleaners have 'miracle' additives, you'll want to avoid these and use pure lye. A solution of lye and water (about three parts water and one part lye) should be brushed on the back and sides of the bow. A word of caution; wear some type of glasses and long sleeves and gloves when handling the lye solution. Lye can burn you just like a strong acid, so be VERY careful not to get it in your eyes or on your skin. After the lye has been brushed on the bow, the wood should be immediately rinsed with boiling water. Rinse the back of the bow, turn it over and rinse the belly, then turn it over again and pour the remaining water on the back.

When the bow has dried from the degreasing procedure, bring it in to where the glue is heating and the sinew will be applied. Brush a thin solution of warm hide glue on the back and sides of the bow. Do not overlook this step of 'sizing' the wood preparatory to putting on the sinew. It seems insignificant, since the sinew is applied with the same glue that is used for sizing, but will make a big difference in how well the sinew adheres to the bow. Once the sizing glue has dried, you are ready to start putting on the much-heralded sinew.

APPLYING SINEW

Your bow has been sized and set on blocks at the front of the workbench. There are thirty or forty bundles of sinew set out at intervals on the work surface. You'll want the bundles to be all different lengths; short, medium, and long. The glue is the right consistency and temperature. It's like thin syrup and very warm to the touch.

You will need something to smooth down the sinew as it is applied. A round dowel rod works fine. I use a piece of buffalo bone, found in a depres-

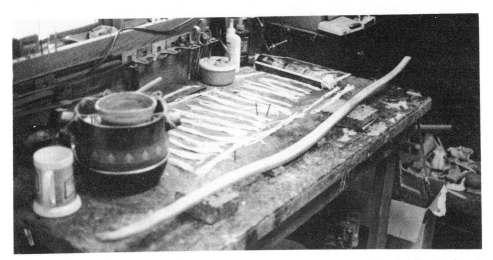

Work bench arranged for putting sinew on bow. Note sinew bundles spread out and magazine at top of bench with more bundles inside.

sion in a line of sandhills on the plains of Texas, but any hard, smooth implement will work. Keep your 'smoother' in a cup of water so the glue won't build up on it.

Grasp one of the longer bundles of sinew in the middle and dip it in the glue. Again, the glue should be very warm, but not uncomfortably hot. Gently

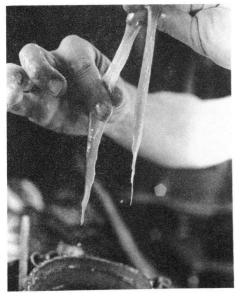

Using fingers to strip excess glue from sinew bundle.

The smoothing tool used to flatten and combine sinew bundles on the bow. Note extra glue being squeezed from the sinew.

swirl the sinew around in the glue until it is completely saturated and limp. This usually takes about thirty seconds. You'll want to switch the sinew to your other hand so the area that was under your fingers can absorb glue, too. Hold the bundle up over the glue pot and squeegee the sinew with your free hand from the center outwards. This flattens the sinew bundle and squeezes out any excess glue. But don't try to squeeze out too much glue, on this first course of sinew to wood contact you want enough glue to give plenty of adhesion.

The first row of sinew should be laid down the center of the bow and will be about half to three-quarters of an inch wide. Place the first bundle at the handle, it should lie across the halfway point of the bow, with half on one limb and half on the other. Use the smoothing tool to flatten and spread out the sinew bundle. Be sure to smooth from the center of the sinew bundle toward the ends, if you start at one end the sinew will get wrinkled up and won't lay flat. Working from the center outwards will also stretch the sinew as it is glued down, which helps impart more of the sinews' tension to the wood. Push down firmly with the smoothing tool to make sure there is good contact between the sinew and the wood.

Continue down the center of the bow with the next bundle. Butt it end to end with the last one you placed and smooth it down. Carry on with this row until you reach the end of the bow, smoothing each bundle as you go. If a bundle of sinew is too long, overlap it around the tip onto the belly of the bow. If a bundle does not quite reach the end, use one of the short bundles to finish the row and overlap the tip. Complete this center row, down the length of the bow from tip to tip.

Glue on your fingers will start to get exceedingly tacky after placing five or ten bundles of sinew. When this happens, wash your hands under warm water and dry them off on an old towel, or keep a pan of warm water on the workbench to rinse your hands.

The hot double boiler will cause water to evaporate from the glue constantly, making it thicker. Every time I rinse my hands, I'll add a splash of warm water to the glue and stir it to keep it the right consistency.

The next row of sinew should start right next to the first, with one end at the middle of the bow. The first row overlapped the middle, so we are starting this row in a different place. The reason for this is to prevent a seam across the bow where the sinew bundles are all spliced together in a line. The bundles should be staggered, like bricks in a wall, with no seam across the bow. Smooth the bundles down as you go, both firmly onto the wood and into the sinew that has already been placed. We're creating a solid matrix of sinew and glue, ideally with no delineation between sinew bundles.

When you get to the side of the bow, continue the sinew over the edge and at least halfway down the side. Having some thin bundles of sinew ready on the workbench is handy if you only need a thin strip to complete the sinew on a side.

After the first course is finished, sinew should entirely cover the back of the bow, overlap the tips, and come halfway down the sides. Some bowyers maintain that the sinew should be allowed to dry between courses, or that two courses should be applied and permitted to dry for a couple of weeks and then another two courses applied. I've tried this method and can see no difference between it and putting the sinew on all at once. In fact, I prefer to place all of the sinew in one application because it's more convenient.

It is easier to finish the sinew, once it's cured, if the back is slightly rounded. Since most staves cut from a large tree are fairly flat on the back, the sinew-backing can be rounded by the way you place the sinew. For the second course, sinew can be laid down the center of the bow in a 1/2" to 3/4" wide strip. The third course can consist of two rows, one down either side of the centerline. The second and third courses will mound up the center of the bow. For the next course, sinew should be placed across the entire back, from one edge to the other. The sinew does not have to be continued down over the sides, as the first course was, but it is fine if you wish to do so. Be sure to continue the sinew out to overlap the ends on each course.

When you have applied the total amount of sinew that you want, check to make sure there are no major valleys or depressions in the back. If there are, they can be filled in with a bundle of sinew that is the appropriate length. The sinew, when wet, will be very thick and it will look as though there is a tremendous backing on the bow. Don't be fooled, for as the sinew dries it will shrink, and will leave a much thinner layer on the finished bow.

Once you are satisfied with the back, completely coat it with a thin solution of hide glue. Just dip a couple of fingers in the glue pot and rub a generous portion over the back and sides of the bow.

The bow is about 70% complete at this point, so you can take a deep breath and relax while the sinew is curing. Don't get too comfortable, though, because this curing interval is a good time to be making bowstrings, arrows, and quivers.

CURING

The freshly sinewed bow can be left on the workbench until the glue has set up. After 24 hours the glue and sinew will be dry on the surface and will only have a slight 'give' when squeezed.

After the initial 24 hour drying period, it is advantageous to place the bow outside if the weather is not damp. The sun will aid in driving moisture from the bow and begin shrinking the stretched sinew fibers. A bow should be brought in at night, so any dew will not slow the drying process.

It is beneficial to place a finished sinew-backed bow in the sun at any time, to shrink the sinew and add speed to its delivery. The ancient Turks, who had such remarkable sinew-backed horn bows, would place their bows in a special oven to drive moisture from them and make them shoot harder.

Anyway, the sinew needs to be allowed to dry for at least ten days, in a dry climate, and fourteen days, or longer, if the weather is damp. You can wait thirty days, or more, if you wish, but the bow can safely be worked in the shorter drying time.

FINISHING

When the drying time is complete, the sinew is smoothed and finished. Ridges that are left in the sinew are scraped out with a knife held at right angles to the bow. The sinew is smoothed exactly as the wood was during the

Scraping out high spots in the cured sinew with a blade held at right angles to the bow.

finishing process described for self bows. After the scraping, a sanding block with 100 grit sandpaper can be used to smooth the back. Don't try to make the back perfectly smooth, just take out the high spots and we'll finish it later.

Sinew that was lapped around onto the belly at the ends should be trimmed off. It can be trimmed right at the end of the bow with a sharp knife, or tapered down to the wood about even with the positioning of the nocks.

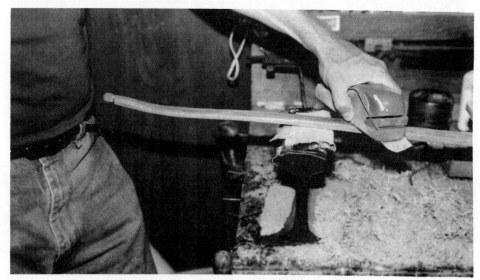

Using a sanding block and 100 grit sandpaper to smooth the sinew.

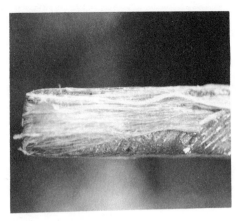
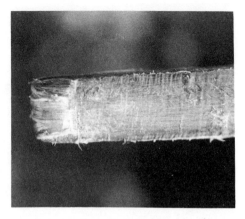

Sinew lapped around onto belly of the bow.

Cured sinew trimmed even with where the nocks will be cut.

At this stage, nocks should be cut in the bow so it can be strung. From this point on, tillering the sinew-backed bow is exactly like tillering the self bow, as described earlier.

There are, however, a couple of additional things you need to be aware of during the tillering process with a sinew-backed bow. First, it is critical to draw a sinewed bow every time wood is removed. This was mentioned at length when tillering a self bow, but it is even more imperative with a sinew-backed bow. The highly tensioned sinew layer has to be stretched before the bow will show the true effects of wood removal. Draw the bow every time you take wood off.

A second point to be aware of is that a sinewed bow may exhibit some ominous creaking sounds the first few times you draw it. The sound is precisely like that of wood cracking and preparing to explode. The heart-stopping sound is not wood cracking, but rather glue cracking on the back of the bow. Not every bow does this, but if yours does, the glue cracking is completely harmless and doesn't hurt anything except your composure.

When the bow is tillered, and it has been shot for a few days, any recurved tips need to be wrapped with sinew. A tip that is not wrapped may eventually have the sinew pull loose from the wood due to the tension of the sinew. The bundles of leg sinew, dipped in glue, can be spiraled around the ends for three or four inches. When the glue dries, this wrapped sinew can be sanded as the entire back was earlier. This sinew-wrapping also needs to be done in the center of a bow that has a deep set-back. Thin, wet rawhide can be used to wrap the center and tips of a bow to hold the sinew down. This rawhide wrapping was quite common on Western yew bows.

To complete the bow, the sinew-back needs to be finished before the wood is sanded and oiled. (If you plan to cover the sinew with a snakeskin, refer at this point to the section on decoration). The scraped and sanded sinew back will usually exhibit some tiny threads of sinew that are loose. There is a simple method for finishing the sinew and sticking down the loose threads. Heat

Bow tips wrapped with sinew. The tip in center was wrapped before snakeskin was applied.

Unwrapped tip showing how sinew back eventually pulled loose.

the pot of hide glue and smear a coat of fairly thin glue on the back and sides. Wait for the glue to get tacky, about five minutes, then rub a wet cloth from the center out to each tip. The result will be a smooth glossy finish.

After the sinew-back is completed, either by smoothing down or adding a snakeskin, the belly and sides are finished as described earlier for a self bow. The ridges are scraped out and the wood sanded and burnished to a polished finish. The wooden belly should be oiled, as for a self bow, but the sinew back should not be. The long-awaited, much sweated over bow is now completed, unless you want to add a handle or other decoration.

Your bow will continue to season over several months, as the sinew dries even further. The reflex in the bow may increase. The weight of the bow may

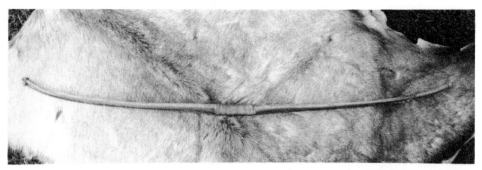

Yew wood bow that was flat before sinew was applied. Sinew has cured for two weeks and given the bow this much reflex.

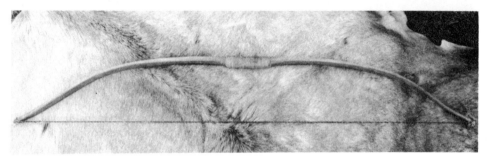

Same bow strung.

increase slightly, too, as the sinew shrinks. If the bow gets too strong, you can always scrape a little more wood from the belly to lighten it.

With a heavy layer of sinew, the continued shrinking may cause some belly cracks. These will look foreboding, since we have spent so much time avoiding cracks, but they do no harm. The cracks simply show that the sinew is doing its work well. I once took a sinew-backed yew wood bow to New Mexico. Leaving the bow in a pickup with the windows rolled up, I left for a week-long cross-country horseback trip. After returning, I discovered that the modest 45# bow, with a thin backing of sinew, had been transformed into a rocket launcher by the dry air and oven-like temperatures in the pickup. The patented 'pickup' treatment had shrunk the sinew and drawn the bow into a backwards 'C' shape. The little bow would deliver a light reed arrow at velocities that were hard to believe. With a soft wood such as yew, or with a severe drying such as the oven-like 'pick-up' treatment the cracks may reach scary proportions. When we first examined the bow, a companion commented that the bow was broken. I did not disagree with him, since the cracks in it were fairly extensive. However, the bow shot much better than it ever had, and I came to realize that the cracks in the belly were not detrimental. They only reflected how much tension the sinew was exerting.

Jay Massey, the fine bowyer and author from Alaska, has another theory about the belly cracks. He maintains that the cracks are caused by moisture from the glue and sinew being absorbed by the dry, seasoned wood. As the

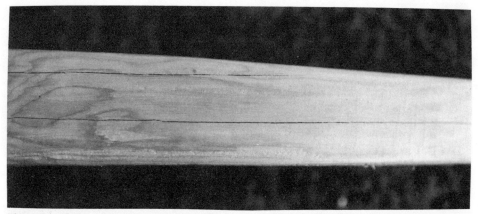

The sinister belly cracks in the yew wood bow.

moisture swells the wood and then dries out on the belly side, it causes cracks. It does seem as if very dry, aged wood is worse about developing belly cracks than fairly green wood. One possible preventative may be to put plastic tape, that the water cannot penetrate, on the belly before the sinew and glue (and water) are applied. When the sinew is dry and cured the tape can be removed and the bow finished. I'm not sure if I don't like Jay's theory as much as mine, but in any case, if your bow develops these cracks we both agree that they do no harm.

COMPOSITE BOWS

A composite bow, made from laminated horn and sinew, seems to hold a fascination for people. Perhaps it's the remarkable performance of composite bows, like the Turkish horn bows that would shoot half a mile, or the fact that a 36" horn bow can be drawn with a 23" arrow, a major overdraw that pulls the bow almost double. Accomplished bowyers sooner or later seem to feel compelled to try a horn bow, usually from bighorn sheep horn. The bighorn sheep bow was the most common Native American composite bow, probably thirty or forty originals still survive in museums and private collections. Several bowyers and authors, among them Laubin, Hamilton, Holm, Massey, and Grayson, have recreated these sheephorn bows and clearly described the process for making one.

Since suitable sheephorns are either impossible or terribly expensive to get, I've always been interested in another type of Native American composite, the buffalo horn bow. To my knowledge, there are no surviving examples of this type of bow either in museums or private collections. The bows were exceedingly rare to begin with, because of the difficulty of making one, and so loaded with prestige I believe the few that existed were buried with their owners when they died. That is why this type of bow became extinct.

My interest was aroused, though, by a passage from the diary of Osborne Russell. In it, Russell describes a group of Shoshone Indians he came across in present day Yellowstone Park in 1835;

"They were well armed with bows and arrows pointed with obsidian the bows were beautifully wrought from Sheep, Buffalo, and Elk horns secured with Deer and Elk sinews and ornamented with porcupine quills and generally about 3 feet long." [4]

I was fascinated with this description and began trying to recreate one of these bows, but the problem with making a buffalo horn bow is that the pieces of horn are too short to cover an entire limb. The Turkish water buffalo horn bows and North American sheep and elk horn bows were made from two pieces spliced at the handle, so each limb was a solid piece of horn. Convinced that the buffalo horn bows were made like the Turkish bows, with a wooden core to hold the horn belly and sinew together, I began to laminate sections of buffalo horn to the wood. Since the longest piece of horn that can be cut is 9 or 10 inches, I used four sections of horn with splices at the center of the bow and halfway out on each limb. After trying a number of different splicing joints, all failures, it occured to me that the horn was only under compression, or being pushed together. It followed that a joint where the two pieces of horn butted up flat against each other would provide the most strength and allow the compression to be applied smoothly. This type of joint worked on the first try.

The first successful bow that I built was 36" long, 1¼" wide at the handle, and 3/4" wide at the tips. It also pulled about 120 pounds and took two of us to get strung. Since there is not really a good way to reduce the sinew or the horn, the bow was clearly too wide. The next attempt, which is pictured in this section and on the front cover of the book, was 7/8" wide at the grip and 1/2" wide at the tips. This bow was more reasonable, and pulled 42 pounds when drawn 23". A bow 1" wide at the handle and with more sinew would probably pull about 50 pounds.

The sections of horn were cut from the outside of four buffalo horns, and then trimmed to size and sanded to about 1/8" thickness. The sections were then boiled to be made flexible. The horns were bent to the same shape as the wood core, which was fashioned and shaped like a mini-bow. The hot horns were quite flexible, so I'm convinced that they can be made to correspond to any shape wooden core. The belly of the wood, as well as the side of the horn that faces the wood, must be made perfectly flat so they will fit together. Any bumps or valleys may cause the glue to come loose under the terrific strain that it has to endure. When the pieces fit snuggly, roughen the surface of the wood and the horn with a hacksaw blade so the glue will have a better grip.

I found that the wood and horn must be degreased just like the wood for a sinew-backed bow, and, as importantly, that the wood and horn must be sized with thin hide glue before being put together. I started at the center of the wood with the first piece of horn after applying a generous portion of glue to both materials. Hide glue must also be placed between the horns, where they butt against each other, so the compression will be equal and even. The horn

---

4. *Russell, Journal of a Trapper (1965, p. 26-27)*

A simple clamp. The object to be held would be placed between jaws at left and the wedge at right driven into the split.

was positioned and held in place with C-clamps on each end. Other clamps were put along the length of the horn to make a tight fit and squeeze out any excess glue. I learned not to tighten the clamps too much, as the glue is all squeezed out resulting in a dry joint that will fail. All four pieces of horn are applied in this manner, and there will be clamps side by side along the length of the wood core when it is complete. Making a bow of this type without modern clamps would be difficult, though not impossible. The horn could be secured with a wrapping of rawhide or string, or a simple wedge clamp could be fashioned that would serve the purpose.

When the glue has dried for at least a week, the clamps are removed and any places where the horn hangs off of the wood core on the sides are evened up. The three joints are then wrapped with sinew dipped in hide glue for an inch on either side of the splice. After the wrapping is dry, about half a day, the wooden core is sinew backed with at least four courses of sinew. Bring the sinew down all the way to the belly of the bow as the wooden core should not be exposed. When the sinew backing is completed, the splices should be wrapped again, and sinew nocks should be built up on either end (see photo at nock section). Season the sinew backing just like the backing for a wooden bow.

Be aware that a slip knot must be used on the string in conjunction with the sinew nocks as a loop in the string would pull off of the end. The first successful bow was slightly out of tiller when I got it strung. I gently steamed the sinew backing on the strong limb and pulled the bow. After about three applications of steam and flexing, the stronger limb relaxed a little, and the bow pulled evenly. The bow has remained tillered ever since so this method works, though you should be careful not to overdo it or the sinew back will be lying on the floor. The sinew back or horn belly could also be scraped to tiller the bow, though this would be difficult to do evenly since the sinew wrappings are around the splices.

Buffalo horn bow, unstrung.

Same bow strung. Note buffalo sinew string and horsehair decoration on tip.

Buffalo horn bow at full draw. The 36" bow is pulled 23", a tremendous overdraw by wooden bow standards.

After all of the failures and trouble, how did the bow shoot? It feels like pulling a big rubber band. The strength increases towards the back of the draw but there was no abrupt intensification in stiffness, or stacking, like is experienced with a wooden bow that is stressed to the limit. In fact, I've only worked up the nerve to draw it back 23", which is almost pulling the bow double, but it feels as if there is enough flexibility in it to be drawn even further. The bow at full draw feels lighter than the 42 pounds, perhaps because its flexibility is deceiving. The little bow shoots hard, extremely hard considering the light poundage. I haven't run comparison tests through a chronograph but feel sure that is would shoot faster than a 42 pound wooden bow.

The buffalo horn bow is clearly a viable weapon, despite all the trouble to make one. Its short length would be a distinct advantage on a horse, or a longer version could be made to take a normal 28" arrow. It would probably be difficult to shoot one well, though, since the proportionally short bow would be unforgiving and amplify any mistakes. Making one is about the ultimate test for a bowyer, however, the end result is a beautiful and striking weapon with the shiny black belly and quillwork decoration. The end result is also very satisfying, since this type of bow was extinct for awhile. They're also fun, as few people can walk past it without stopping to look at the pretty "kid's" bow.

The success of the buffalo horn bow made me brave, and I next attempted a buffalo rib bow. After obtaining a box of fresh buffalo ribs, I soon discovered that there is a twist in the ribs, as well as the expected curve. The thirteenth ribs back from the front were the straightest, so I decided to try them. The ribs are considerably longer than buffalo horns, so it looked as if three pieces would make a bow. The pieces from the inside of the ribs formed each limb while a section from the outside of a rib was turned over to form the backset handle section. The ribs were split in half and the porous center of the bone scraped down to solid material. This left about 1/8" thickness of bone.

The bone, when finally shaped, was flexible, but not nearly so flexible as the buffalo horn had been. Boiling didn't help much, either. So I did this bow backwards from the earlier one, instead of shaping the bone to the wooden core, I heated the wood and shaped it to the bone. The dimensions for this bow are 36" long, 7/8" at the handle, and 5/8" at the tips.

The bone was very greasy so I treated it with lye and boiling water twice to make sure the glue would stick. Again, I had to make sure that the wooden core and bone sections were perfectly flat, to ensure a good fit. After sizing the wood and bone with the thin glue solution, I glued the three pieces of bone to the wood using clamps much like had been done before with the buffalo horn sections. When the glue was dry the clamps were removed and the joints wrapped with sinew. The wooden core was then sinew-backed and the joints again wrapped. Sinew nocks were built up on each limb. The bow was cured for two weeks before a string was put on it.

The bow, when first strung, had a pleasing Cupid's bow shape to it. I got a real shock, though, when pulling and working the bow up to its draw length of 23", since I expected a rubber band flexibility like with the buffalo horn bow. The rib bow was stiff and contrary, and after a draw of about 19" stacked up and wouldn't pull any further. When a bow loses its flexibility it is trying

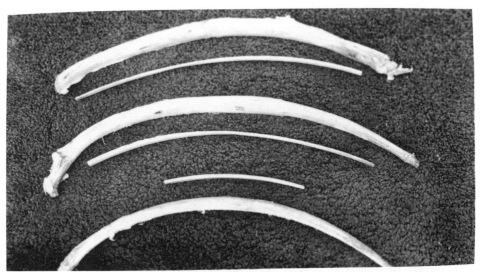

Buffalo ribs showing sections of bone that can be cut from them.

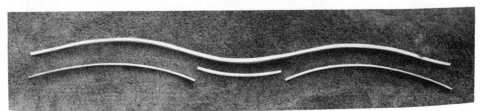

Rib sections aligned with wooden core.

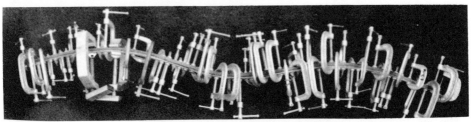

Rib bow after gluing, with clamps holding bone sections to wooden core.

Two pieces of rib with a flat splice. This is the same splice that was used on the buffalo horn bow.

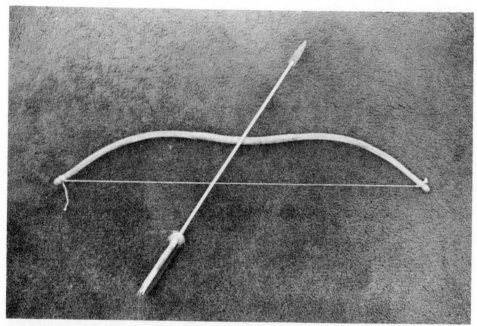

Completed buffalo rib bow. The bow is 36" long and the arrow 23".

to tell you something, and that's if you pull it any further it's going to explode. For once, I didn't push my luck, but continued working the bow at shorter draw lengths. The bow pulled pretty well until that point at 19" was reached, then the full compression of the bone was met and it would suddenly stop bending.

The bow pulled a surprising 48 pounds at only a 19" draw, though the speed with which it shot an arrow was not remarkable. I'm sure a good osage orange bow of the same weight would out-perform it. The bow has a beautiful shape, though it is not particularly pleasant to shoot due to its stiffness.

My conclusions about the rib bow are less charitable than those about the buffalo horn bow. Although the bone will make a bow, it is almost more trouble than it is worth. The advantage of the composite bow, the tremendous overdraw, does not exist with a rib bow. The rib bow is indeed a novelty, as there are probably not more than one or two others in existence, but the time and effort put into it could be more profitably used to make a good sheep or buffalo horn bow.

The composite bows, no matter what materials are being used, make pretty, unusual bows. The sheep and buffalo horns especially make good bows, giving a long draw and terrific speed. Aside from the challenge of making them, however, there is not really much practical application, outside of using them from horseback or flight shooting for distance. The incredibly short bows are difficult to shoot accurately, but somehow I still like them, and have plans for a buffalo horn bow made from five sections of horn. The bow will be 45" long and draw a 29" arrow. I only hope it doesn't pull 120 pounds.

DECORATION

SNAKESKIN

A snakeskin covering is a practical addition to a sinew-backed bow. The Indians added this feature to their bows occasionally, but it was not common. They probably didn't like messing with a rattlesnake. But they sometimes used it, as I have seen a few sinew-backed bows from the Northern Plains and the West Coast which employed it.

The snakeskin gives the bow a nice touch, but it is also useful for several reasons. First of all, it helps protect and waterproof the sinew. Since the hide glue is water-soluble, on a really damp day the sinew-backing will become slightly tacky. Without a snakeskin, this causes the bow to get dirty. On a damp day, an unprotected bow will also lose a little of its speed, and the snakeskin helps prevent that.

Another important role the snakeskin plays is for camouflage, and there is nothing more effective. If you are a bowhunter who wants to disappear and get close to your game, I recommend that you take advantage of this natural camouflage.

From a purely aesthetic standpoint the snakeskin is beautiful. The patterns and contrasts of the skin, no matter what type of snake you use, are pleasing to the eye. The snakeskin also gives the bow a deadly appearance. A personal favorite is a diamondback rattlesnake skin on an osage orange bow. The highly outlined pattern of the diamonds against the bright yellow of the wood is striking and unforgettable.

Any type of snakeskin can be used, though one with some contrast within it will be more attractive. Snakes such as rattlesnakes, copperheads, corn snakes, and bull snakes are all good. A fresh snake is easy to skin, just split it up the belly and peel the hide off. Of course, with a poisonous snake, you should be very, very, careful with the head. It is best to cut the head off and bury it before attempting to skin the snake. The hide can be put on the bow fresh, or the hide can be frozen or dried until it is ready for use. A tanned hide could also be used, although I would avoid one that had been tanned with glycerine, since it would prevent the glue from adhering to the hide.

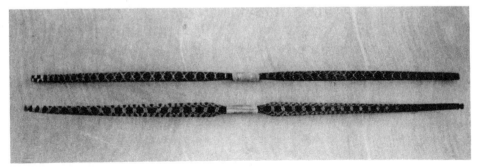

Top bow is covered with two small rattlesnake skins joined at the handle. Note how small diamonds fit nicely on the bow. Bottom bow is backed with a single large bullsnake skin.

Two small rattlesnake skins spliced at the handle.

The fresh, thawed, or soaked and reconstituted dried hide is put on the bow with the same hide glue that holds the sinew on. The bow should be tillered and the sinew scraped and smooth, although the belly and sides should still be rough and unfinished. I like to cut off the thick skin from the belly of a snakehide before putting it on the bow. This belly skin will be down either side of the hide, but be careful not to cut off so much that the hide is too narrow to completely cover the back and sides of the bow.

Consider how the snakeskin will be placed on the bow. It is preferable to have the tail end of the snake on the bottom limb, because of the way the scales lay on the hide. With a rattlesnake hide, the black and white 'coon tail' that is next to the rattles is attractive when placed on the lower tip. A hide that has a diamond pattern, such as a rattlesnake, will look better if two small snakes are used instead of one big one. That is because a snake big enough to cover the entire bow will have a diamond pattern so big it will hang off of the bow and be lost. With two smaller snakeskins, joined at the handle, the diamonds will be small enough to fit exactly on the back of the bow. If using two skins, be careful about matching the color and pattern. There is a remarkable difference in the color between different snakes, so it is best if you can choose the snakes 'on the hoof,' so to speak, and pick two which match.

Place the snakeskin, or skins, flesh side up on the workbench next to the bow. Rub a thin coating of warm hide glue all over the back and sides of the bow with your fingers. Next, rub the hide glue on the flesh side of the snakeskin, being careful not to miss any spots. Start at one end and turn the snakeskin over and onto the bow. Line up the tail of the snakeskin on the lower tip.

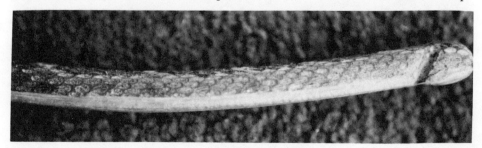

Snakeskin is trimmed off about halfway down the side of the bow.

Work toward the upper limb, straightening the skin and sticking it to the back and sides, while pushing out air bubbles that are trapped under the skin. The glue will dry slowly while trapped between snakeskin and bow, so you have plenty of time to restraighten the hide and get all of the air bubbles out.

When the hide is where you want it, place the bow aside for several hours until the glue begins to set. After the glue gets firm, and the snakeskin won't move, the excess skin that is hanging down past the belly must be trimmed off. Start at one end with a razorblade knife and slice the hide, using the side of the bow for a backstop. I like to trim the snakeskin even with the edge of the sinew, about halfway down the side of the bow, so some wood will show on the side in contrast with the skin. There is no reason you can't trim the hide flush with the belly of the bow if you prefer. When the cut down the side is completed, peel off the excess hide.

Let the bow cure at least a week, to wait for the glue to dry completely, and then finish it according to the instructions for a self bow. The snakeskin backing can be lightly oiled just as the wood can, but be aware that the hide will shed some 'surface' scales when you rub on it. Losing these scales will not damage the hide or change its appearance.

HANDLES

Another useful addition to a bow is a buckskin handle. The handle will keep your hand off of the sinew back, this prevents the moisture in your skin from making the glue tacky. A soft leather handle will also make the bow shoot

Handles, L. to R., buckskin sewn on back, buckskin sewn on side, long buckskin thong wrapped around bow, cloth secured with buckskin wrapping, long cloth strip wrapped around bow.

more quietly. If you plan to kill a buffalo from the back of a thundering horse, a quiet shot will probably not be too important. However, to shoot a deer, a quiet shot becomes essential to prevent them from jumping out of the way of the arrow.

There are several types of handles that you can choose from. First, a piece of leather can be cut to fit the bow. This leather is stitched together on the back or on the off-side of the bow. The off-side is the side away from where the arrow lies across the handle.

Another type of grip is a long buckskin thong, 1/4" to 1/2" wide which is wrapped around and around the bow. The thong can be tied off at one end or stitched down with thread. Either of these first types, sewn or wrapped, can be done with damp rawhide if you prefer.

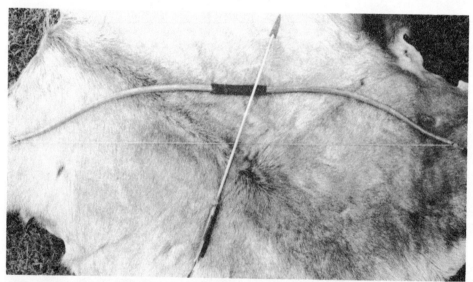

Plains-style bow with cloth wrapped handle.

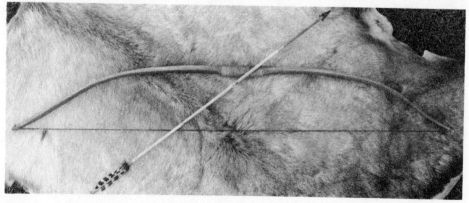

West Coast yew bow with buckskin wrapped handle.

Otter fur 'silencer' on tip of yew bow. These were used on the West Coast.

Cloth can be used for a handle, either stitched on or wrapped around the bow like buckskin. The cloth can also be fastened by wrapping it with leather. I once saw a bow in a museum that had a cloth handle wrapped and secured with an extra bowstring, a slick idea.

There was an interesting addition made to many Western yew bows, and while it is not exactly related to the handle it was useful, nonetheless. A strip of fur about an inch wide was sewn just below the knock, where the string would rest on it. The fur, either mink or otter, acted as a string 'silencer,' and dampened the twang when an arrow was released. This is an important consideration for people who lived by killing deer, since deer are quick enough to dodge out of the way when they hear the unusual sound of a bowstring. Deer, as a friend of mine says, were born with a nervous breakdown. Any experienced bowhunter can tell stories of deer 'jumping the string' before an arrow could arrive. The fur string silencers are a keen, traditional trick to increase hunting success.

While on the subject, the Western Indians also used another type of string silencer on their bows. They would tie bundles of small feathers to the string near the nocks at each end. The feathers would also be decoration, since blue jay and woodpecker were employed.

HORSEHAIR, QUILLWORK, ETC.

There are some items which were put on bows, primarily on the Plains, purely for decoration. If you want to really personalize your bow, consider adding some horsehair or quillwork.

A horsehair tassle was sometimes added to the tip of the upper limb. This was common on the plains and especially on the Southern Plains. The majority of Comanche and Kiowa bows had a carved out wooden tip on the ends that was used to secure the horsehair. On a self bow you can leave a wooden tip, as shown, but on a sinew-backed bow an easier method is to finish the bow, then drill a small hole in the end and glue in a piece of wood to hold the horsehair. The hair is attached to the stick by wrapping it with sinew. The most common colors of hair used in the old days were a natural white, dyed yellow, and dyed red. These colors are a good choice for a modern bow, too.

I have seen two examples of Comanche bows which were incised, or carved,

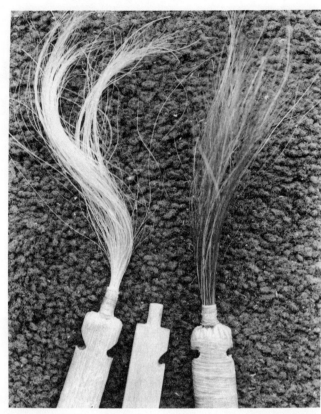

Horsehair decorations. Bow in center shows wooden nub for attaching hair.

on the belly. One, in the Smithsonian's storage, had two 3″ long arrows scratched into the wood on each limb. The other, in a museum in Ft. Worth, Texas, had a pattern of triangles and lines carved on the belly. The incised designs were then painted red and blue. This is a striking decoration, but was most unusual. A customer once had me recreate a Northeastern-style bow, which had six incised circles on the belly. The circles, three per limb, were each the size of a dime. They started at the handle and were about two inches

Porcupine quillwork on horn bow. This bow is shown in color on the front cover.

apart, with the carved area painted red. The red circles on the bright yellow osage orange made an interesting combination.

I have seen one original sinew-backed bow that had a double row of brass tacks down the belly from end to end. A total of 44 tacks were used. This is a decoration that I would use very judiciously, since the tacks would have a tendency to split the wood.

A beautiful decoration for a bow is quillwork, which was occasionally done by the Northern Plains Indians. The quillwork can be placed on both ends of the handle or halfway between the handle and tip on either limb. The technique for quilling a bow is known as 'plaited' quillwork, and is the same one used to put quillwork on pipestems. I won't go into detail about how to do the quillwork, as there are several good books available on the subject (and also, too, because I don't have the first idea how to do it, as my wife is the quillworker of the family).

Another option for a traditional decoration is a strip of cloth, preferably red wool, that is wrapped with fine brass wire. Two of these decorations are used, one on each limb, halfway between the handle and the tip. The wire is wrapped around and around the cloth for about an inch, then the cloth is fringed for another inch or so where it comes out from under the wire. A decoration like this would have been found on Northern Plains bows.

One decoration I have seen on a couple of Sioux bows was the neck skin of a mallard wrapped around the bow at each end of the handle. The iridescent green feathers were a pretty, unusual decoration.

The most beautifully decorated bow I have ever seen was made by a Blackfoot man from the Northern Plains. The bow was short, about 40 inches long, and backed with sinew. Over the sinew was the skin of a Western Garter

Brass wire wrapped around red wool cloth. This decoration would be placed halfway between the handle and each tip.

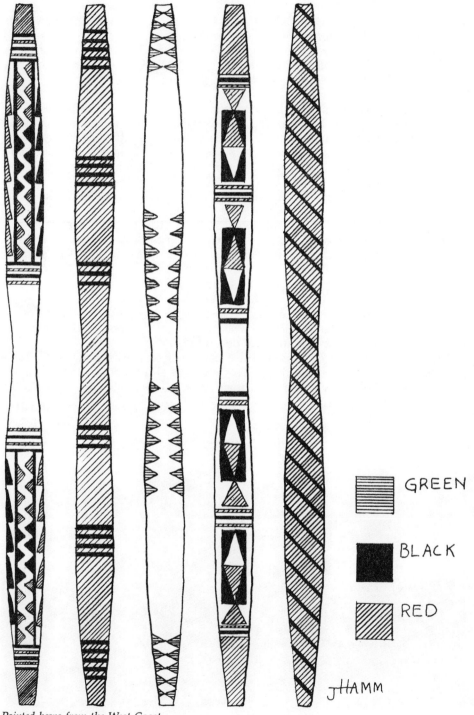

GREEN

BLACK

RED

JHAMM

Painted bows from the West Coast.

Snake, a dark colored snake with an orange stripe running the length of the body. The orange stripe ran down the center of the bow, from tip to tip. The handle was very thin rawhide, cut in a narrow strip and wrapped around and around the bow. Halfway between the handle and each tip was purple and yellow quillwork wrapped over otter fur. The fur was fringed on each side of the quillwork to a length of about four inches. The bow was exquisite, and is a good example of what decoration can do for a weapon.

PAINTED DESIGNS

Most of the painted bows I have examined came from the Indians of the West Coast. The majority of their sinew-backed wood bows were painted in some type of geometric design. The predominate color was red, combined with black or green. To recreate one of these designs, acrylic paint is the best choice. This paint is available in a tube from craft supply stores, and comes in traditional earth colors. It is water soluble, which means it is thinned and cleaned with water, and also can be thinned enough to give the faded color of the original natural paints. Once the acrylic paint dries water does not affect it, unlike tempera paint or some of the powdered paints.

The painted designs are beautiful, but they can serve a practical purpose as well. The geometric designs tend to break up the outline of the bow and serve as camouflage. The sinew-backing of the bow should be smoothed and finished before it is painted. I have seen references to Western Indians coating the back of a finished bow with a combination of hide glue and finely powdered white clay or limestone. This would provide a white background for the painted design and might be something to experiment with. I have also examined a Crow Indian bow, from the Northern Plains, which had the sinew back finished off with a mixture of white powdered clay and hide glue.

Most of the painted bows come from the West, but a few others were painted, as well. The incised designs on the belly of a bow were sometimes painted, as mentioned earlier. The Northern Plains Indians, and especially the Sioux, occasionally painted the belly and sides of a sinew-backed bow. The light colored hickory and ash bows were painted red, and there are numerous examples of this, although it was by no means universal. Bows of this type usually had built-up sinew nocks, instead of nocks cut into the wood. Pre-Columbian Pueblo bows were sometimes painted with bands of black, red, or green. A few of these bows were painted the same color all over.

I have seen two bows which had one side scalloped, with the scalloped edge painted. One was collected by Maximillian in the 1830's, and was identified as Woodland Indian. The scalloped edge was on the right side of the bow, opposite the arrow, and was painted red. The other example of this type of bow was from the Field Museum in Chicago, and was labeled Potawatomi. The scallops were alternately painted red and blue.

If recreating a specific tribal or regional bow, I believe you should remain as true as possible to the materials and decorations of that area. A sinew-backed Sioux-style bow, for example, would look strange if painted with a West Coast Indian design. By the same token, a wide, thin yew wood bow wrapped in quillwork, and with incised designs on the belly, would be somewhat out of place.

STRINGS

Bowstrings from natural materials have always been considered the weak link in Native American archery equipment, and in some ways it's true. The strings made from animal materials are affected by moisture which makes them stretch. Most of the cordage made from plant fiber is not strong enough to take the shock of the bow. A good string is also tedious to make, though there's a trick to it that we'll get to shortly.

Making strings from natural materials should not be considered a lost cause, however, as good, durable strings can be made. The vast majority of bowstrings I have examined were a two-ply string made with a reverse wrapped method. I have seen a few three-ply strings and even saw one where the sinew was plaited into a square string. The best and easiest to make, though, is the two-ply.

It was always difficult for me to make the two-ply reverse wrapped sinew strings like the Native Americans used. They were never even, but had lumps and thin spots throughout the length where splices of new sinew strands were made. I finally discovered the secret to making a uniform string when making cordage out of the thin fibers of yucca. The trick is not to use two large pieces that are half the diameter of the string, but to use many small threads in each half that are constantly being replenished. I tried this with a sinew string, and instead of using one or two pieces of sinew for each half of the string, stripped the sinew down to fine threads and used eight or ten threads per half. I staggered the lengths where only one or two threads would run out and have to be spliced at a time, and the result was a strong, even string with no weak places or lumps. No matter what kind of material you are using for a string, if it has to be spliced, work the fibers down very fine and it will make a better string.

The two-ply reverse wrapped method is not difficult, though it will take a little practice to twist both halves of the string evenly. In fact, it would probably be better to learn on a material that didn't have to be spliced, like a waxed thread such as artificial sinew or commercial bowstring thread. For strings made out of these materials, I'll use four or five threads per half, or a total of eight or ten. Divide the threads into two equal halves and hold the ends between the thumb and forefinger of the left hand (if you're right handed). A knot can be used to tie all of the ends together, if you wish. Grasp half of the string between the fingers of your right hand, within a couple of inches of your left hand, and twist them clockwise. When they are tight, hold them between the thumb and forefinger of the right hand, and using the little and ring fingers of the same hand, reach under and grasp the other half of the string. Twist your right hand counterclockwise and use the fingers of the left hand to secure the twist that is put into the string. Repeat the process with the other half of the string. Quite simply, what is being done is to twist the individual halves clockwise, and to twist them around each other counterclockwise. This wraps them upon themselves so they will not unravel.

Once the basic technique is mastered, some natural materials can be used. The very best strings are made from sinew, as it's the strongest and has just enough stretch to "give" when it has to absorb the jar of the bow. A string

Twist half of the string tightly between the thumb and forefinger of the right hand.

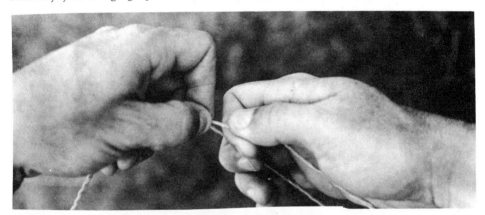

Reach under with the fingers and grasp the other half of the string.

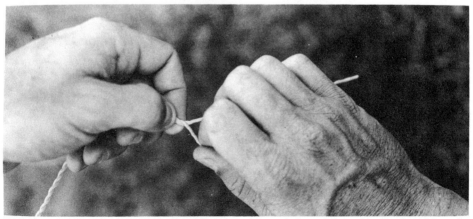

Turn the entire hand counterclockwise, this wraps the two halves of the string together. Move the thumb and forefinger of the left hand up to hold the latest wrap.

from sinew is durable but it can be ruined by too much moisture, but so can the sinew backing on a bow and the feathers on arrows attached with sinew and hide glue. So I never use these weapons in the rain, anyway.

Back sinew from an animal is good for strings because it can be reduced to long, thin pieces. Leg sinew also works well because it is soft and easy to twist up. I've come to prefer buffalo sinew, because it is long and strips out into fine, soft threads. A long piece of deer sinew is good, also. Elk sinew has the length, although it is sometimes stiff and difficult to work.

When you need to splice a new piece in, it should be laid in the Y between the two halves with about 1/4" extending beyond the fork. Hold it in place with the fingers of the left hand and twist the upper half of the string tightly. Lay it over the splice and the other half like is normally done, this holds the new piece in place and locks it in. Now twist the other half of the string, along with the new piece, and twist it around the other half as before. After about two wraps the new piece of sinew has become an integral part of the string. It will take a little practice to be able to judge when more threads should be added to the string, sometimes a new thread is added every wrap.

When the string is finished, the ends of the spliced threads should be sticking out evenly all over it. The ends are trimmed off with scissors and the string secured on each end and stretched between two points. A very thin solution of hide glue is used to rub the string, or saliva can be used, if you prefer. This moisture helps to "melt" the individual fibers together, and since the sinew has a natural glue in it the string will stick together and become much more durable. While the string is damp, turn one end counterclockwise several times to twist the string up tight. The string is then stretched snugly between the two points, but don't pull too hard as the wet string can be pulled in two. A neat trick I've discovered at this stage is to roll the damp string between two flat, smooth surfaces. This presses the threads together even more

Finished buffalo sinew string, top, and a sinew string under construction with splices throughout its length.

and makes the string rounder and smoother than before. I believe most Native American strings were treated in this way as they show to have been flattened and pressed together when damp. When the string dries completely any stiff ends of sinew that protrude can be cleanly removed with fingernail clippers.

Although sinew makes the best strings, some other animal products will make usable ones. The intestines of a deer, cleaned inside and out, make a string that doesn't have to be spliced. It is twisted together with the same reverse wrap technique. The Cherokees made good strings such as this from twisted bear gut. The Choctaws made strings out of squirrel gut twisted up into six-plies. Thin rawhide, which is thoroughly soaked first, will also make a string that needs no splices.

Hair produces a good string, although it's not as strong as might be expected and has to be made larger to withstand the pop of a heavy bow. Horsehair works the best because of its length, although almost any type of hair will work. All animal strings, except hair, are affected by moisture to some extent.

If you use a bow in an area with a lot of rain and dampness, and want to use traditional, natural materials, then a plant fiber string may be the answer. The only plant fiber that I've found suitable for a bowstring was yucca, though I've tried milkweed (a lot of trouble, as the fibers are short), the inner bark of cedar (not strong enough), and nettle (it works, but difficult and time consuming to prepare). I've seen some superb cordage made from the inner bark of a Basswood tree, but it's not native to this area and I've never been able to try it for a bowstring.

The yucca fiber comes from the long leaves of the plant and enough for a bowstring can be stripped out in less than thirty minutes. An entire leaf is split into fourths and the sections pulled across a blade held at right angles to

L. to R., deer gut, rawhide, commercial waxed thread, yucca, elk sinew, buffalo sinew.

it. I usually hold the yucca on my thumb and press the knife blade down against it. This removes the green pulp of the leaf and leaves the long fibers intact. The fibers can be used green, but will not stay tightly wrapped together as they dry. It is better to let the fibers dry for a couple of weeks or so, then moisten them to make them flexible before twisting (I use a primitive Windex bottle filled with water). The fibers then will stay tightly twisted together. I've made a number of strings from yucca and the results were quite satisfactory. Though the yucca is not indestructable, it is durable enough for a lot of shooting and is not affected by moisture. The few plant fiber strings on original bows that I have seen were apparently made from yucca.

KNOTS

Attaching the hard-won string to the bow is the next step. Traditional bows had the string tied fast to the bottom limb. A modern knot which is useful for this is the timber hitch, and though I've never seen a Native American bowstring with this knot it's one you should know.

Most original bows used a series of half-hitches to secure the string, but the best knot I've seen is shown in the photo. This traditional knot was on the beautiful Blackfoot bow that I described in the section on bow decoration, and is the one I've come to use almost exclusively with natural strings.

Two modern knots. A plaited loop for the top limb, left, and the timber hitch for attaching the string to the bottom limb.

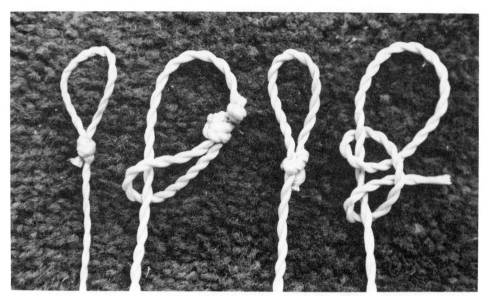

Native American knots. L. to R., an overhand knot tied in string to make a loop, end of string passed through loop of overhand knot to form a slip knot, slip knot formed by tying string back to itself, and an excellent knot for attaching the string to the bottom limb.

The upper end of Native American strings usually had a slip knot arrangement to go in the nocks. The slip knot could be made by tying the string back upon itself. Most were done in this way. A slip knot was also made by tying an overhand loop in the string, then passing the other end of the string through it. Yet another method was to plait a loop in the end of the string, not to put over the nocks, but for the other end of the string to pass through to form a slip knot. I'm not sure why they preferred the slip knots, as a loop is much easier to get out of the nocks when unstringing the bow. This is probably why the single upper nock is common on the plains, as it was easier to get a slip knot out of than a double nock. A slip knot was the norm across the country so for the re-creation of an original bow it's the one to use.

I have only seen a very few original bows where a loop was used to go into the nocks on the upper limb. An overhand knot was tied in the string to yield a loop, and this simple arrangement was, to my mind, an improvement on the usual slip knot. This was used occasionally on the West Coast and rarely upon the Plains. An even better, though more difficult, loop can be made by plaiting the twisted string back into itself. I've seen this done twice on Indian bows, once on a Paiute sheephorn bow where the other end of the string was stuck through the loop to make a slip knot, and once on a Comanche bow where the plaited loop was actually used to go into double nocks on the bow. This second bow was typically Comanche except for the unusual string arrangement.

Though a plaited loop and double nocks were rare on original bows, it is an excellent method for stringing a bow. The plaited loop is made by twisting a

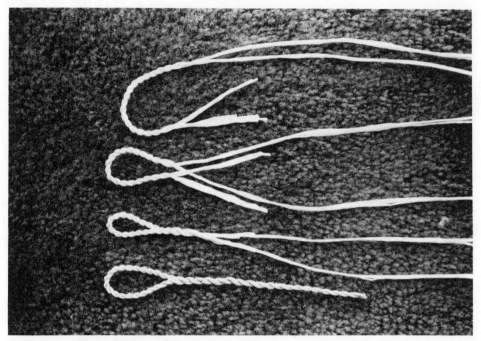

Sequence for making the plaited loop.

section of the string long enough to make the loop. After forming the loop, the two tails on the end of it are twisted together with the two main sections of string. This makes a neat loop that will not come undone and absorbs the stress of the bow evenly throughout its length. This type of loop can be put into a sinew or yucca fiber string and works very well.

There are a lot of options for making strings and knots, and any of these methods can be used with modern threads. If you are going to use the synthetics, I'd recommend the artificial sinew, or waxed thread. It is strong, and with the wax has the appearance of a natural fiber. If you have mastered the task of making one out of synthetics, though, you can make a good string from sinew or some other natural material. A well-made wooden bow always seems happier when it has a sinew string on it.

Part 2

ARROWS

And now, I hope you're ready for some REALLY bad news. Making the bow was the easiest part of this whole deal. Building well-balanced, good-shooting arrows is an art, plain and simple. It's also time consuming. You can plan on spending a total of, at the very least, half a day on each arrow, if you make them from scratch. While you'll probably be able to make a nice bow after just a few tries, arrowmaking will only come to you after many dozens of attempts.

But before you throw this book and decide to take up something simple, like Nuclear Fusion for Fun and Profit, there are some real benefits to making arrows. First of all, a handmade arrow is a thing of beauty, there's nothing prettier or deadlier looking. Another reason to make your own is that they fly as true as anything you can buy in a store. Shooting an aluminum arrow from a handmade wooden bow would be almost sacrilegious, anyway, so you need to learn how to make arrows.

Like anything truly worth knowing, arrowmaking takes time and considerable effort. If it was easy and could be learned in thirty minutes it wouldn't be a challenge. If you're like me, and you must be to some degree to have stayed along to this point, if arrowmaking could be mastered in an afternoon you probably wouldn't be interested.

One glance at a well-made arrow tells you that its maker is a meticulous craftsman, a man you can learn from no matter how skilled you eventually become. A while back, after I had been making bows and arrows professionally for several years, a Comanche man called to ask about some osage orange. He and his son came to visit, and while I was impressed with the bows that he brought, when he showed me his arrows it blew my socks off. I was already making decent arrows, but I learned a great deal more about arrows from him and we've remained close friends to this day. Looking at a man's arrows will tell you the true story of the kind of craftsman and weapons maker he is.

REGIONAL STYLES

Arrows tended to evolve along regional lines, much like the bows did. This had to do with available materials, the way the arrows were used, and to some degree with the sharing of information and arrowmaking techniques.

As a very general rule, the Indians who hunted on foot made longer and more accurate arrows than those who hunted and fought from horseback. The Indians who hunted and stalked their game on foot, in the eastern part of the country and on the West Coast, usually got just one shot, so their arrows had to be very carefully made to be as accurate as possible. They made longer bows and arrows, as well, which made the weapons easier to shoot accurately. As a group, the most beautiful, well-made original arrows I have ever exam-

Eastern-style arrows. Top to bottom; sinew wrapped feathers with no glue (dogwood shaft), three whole feathers wrapped with sinew at each end (yaupon shaft), wing feathers attached with sinew and hide glue (reed shaft), and Cherokee-style fletch using two whole feathers and no glue (reed shaft).

ined came from the West Coast. The shafts are remarkably straight even after all this time. The fletching has been carefully applied and the arrows are often still in a shootable condition. Virtually all of the Western arrows that I have examined show this careful workmanship, so it was clearly a widespread regional necessity to make excellent, accurate arrows.

The Plains Indians were not burdened with having to make a single long range, pin-point accurate shot. They could ride up within ten feet of a buffalo and loose as many arrows as necessary to bring him down. Their arrows reflected this by being short, 22" to 26", and usually expediently made, more than adequate to do the job at hand but without the painstaking work of the Western Indians. This is not to say that the Plains arrowmakers did not understand how to make excellent arrows, as there are many examples, from many Plains tribes, showing well-balanced, beautifully made and decorated arrows. Fine, original Plains arrows are not unusual, but they were not necessary to sustain life and so were in the minority.

Most of the Plains tribes used a distinctive, "raised" nock that was larger than the rest of the arrow. This large nock aided in the pinch-type release that the people of that area used. The nock gave more of a purchase for the gripping fingers and allowed the arrow to be pulled further. More on this in the Shooting section.

The Plains people generally used longer feathers for their arrows than was common for people who hunted on foot. The Eastern and Western Indians usually cut their feathers short enough so that they would not touch the bow when an arrow was placed on the string. There were two reasons for this. First, if the feathers were resting on the bow in the nocked position, they would make noise when pulled across the bow as the arrow was drawn. A deer is one big radar antenna, looking for something trying to eat him, so the slightest sound of feathers scraping across a bow could well make the difference between a successful hunt and starving to death. Another reason for the

West Coast-style arrows. Top to bottom; wing feathers attached with sinew at each end and no glue (reed shaft), tail feathers with sinew at each end and no glue (reed shaft), wing feathers attached with sinew at each end and hide glue (dogwood shaft).

Plains-style arrows. Top, wing feather attached with sinew wrapping at each end as well as hide glue (chokecherry shaft), tail feather with sinew wrapping and no glue (salt cedar shaft).

shorter feathers was that the feathers got distorted when forced to lay across the bow for long periods of time, and naturally, this decreases accuracy. The Plains tribes, who weren't forced to make silent or perfectly accurate shots, were able to use longer feathers to stabilize their arrows. As a rule, people who hunted on foot, both East and West, cut their feathers short enough to clear their bows.

There are many other regional characteristics of arrows, having to do with the way they are fletched and decorated, as well as with the types of points

Arrow Averages

REGION AND TRIBE	SHAFT MATERIAL	SHAFT LENGTH	SHAFT DIAMETER	FEATHER LENGTH	POINTS IN ORDER OF USAGE
WEST COAST YAHI, HUPA, SHASTA	WITCH HAZEL, DOGWOOD, VIBURNUM	26″ - 29″	¼ - ⁷⁄₁₆″	3-6″ MOSTLY 5-6″	OBSIDIAN FLINT STEEL
	REED	26″; 3-8″ FORESHAFT	REED ⅜″; ⁷⁄₁₆″ LARGE END		
GREAT BASIN SHOSHONE, PAIUTE	CHOKECHERRY SERVICEBERRY	24-30″	¼ - ⁵⁄₁₆″	3-7″	OBSIDIAN FLINT STEEL
	REED	26-29″; 4-7″ FORESHAFT	⅜ - ⁷⁄₁₆″		
SOUTHWEST APACHE, NAVAJO	DOGWOOD	22 - 24″	⁹⁄₃₂″	4 - 7″	FLINT STEEL
	REED	23 - 26″; 5-7″ FORESHAFT	REED ⁷⁄₁₆ - ½″ LARGE END	5 - 6″	
SOUTHERN PLAINS COMANCHE, KIOWA	DOGWOOD	22 - 26″	¼ - ⁵⁄₁₆″	5 - 7″	STEEL, VERY RARELY BONE
NORTHERN PLAINS SIOUX, CROW, BLACKFOOT	RED OSIER DOGWOOD, WILD ROSE, CHOKECHERRY	22 - 25″	¼ - ⁵⁄₁₆″	5 - 8″	STEEL, VERY RARELY BONE
UPPER MIDWEST SAUK & FOX, CHIPPEWA, POTAWATOMI	DOGWOOD, VIBURNUM, WITCH HAZEL	24 - 29″	⁵⁄₁₆ - ⁷⁄₁₆″	3 - 6″	FLINT, STEEL, VERY RARELY COPPER
EAST COAST IROQUOIS, POWHATAN, CHEROKEE	DOGWOOD, YAUPON, WITCH HAZEL, VIBURBUM	26 - 29″	⅜ - ⁷⁄₁₆″	4 - 6″	FLINT BONE STEEL, VERY RARELY BRASS
	REED	25 - 32″ FORESHAFT NOT ALWAYS USED	⅜″		

used. We'll cover these variations in the sections dealing with the different parts of the arrow. Also note the graph detailing the averages for arrows from various parts of the country.

WOODEN ARROWSHAFTS

Obtaining a nice, straight, even shaft which will stay straight is about 70% of the arrowmaking battle. After the shafts are made, the rest of the process is downhill. An acceptable way to make arrows is to use commercial wooden shafts, then fletch them by hand. This speeds up the process a great deal and shouldn't offend your bow. Making truly traditional arrows, though, begins with cutting your own shafts.

TYPES OF WOOD

A good wooden arrowshaft has to have several properties. It needs to be flexible but stiff. It has to have grown relatively straight, and just as important, once it is straightened will stay straight. No wooden arrowshaft, commercial or otherwise, will stay perfectly straight through changes in temperature and humidity. The better natural shafts will not warp badly, however, and will just require periodic minor straightening. When the arrows are being used and checked daily, as on a hunting trip, they remain straight and seldom need correcting.

One of the best natural materials is dogwood which grows in many species throughout the country. Dogwood is very hard, even harder than osage orange, and grows in thickets with finger sized saplings reaching for the sunlight. Dogwood also straightens easily and remains straight. The wood is so hard that it will take a high polish, yielding a beautiful shaft. On the Southern Plains the Comanches and Kiowas used dogwood almost exclusively, as it grew in the eastern part of their country. The people of the Northern Plains, the Sioux, Cheyenne, Crow and Blackfoot, used a type of dogwood called Red Osier. Dogwood was utilized in the Eastern part of the country and on the

Bundles of shafts. Top to bottom; dogwood, salt cedar, and yaupon.

West Coast as well. It seems to have been made into arrows by Native Americans anywhere it was found, and is still an excellent choice today.

Yaupon Holly was used for arrows throughout its range in the Southeast and northward to Virginia. A dense wood, it will take a nice polish and also stays straight. I've used it for hunting arrows and was quite satisfied with the results.

Viburnum grows throughout the eastern half of the country and right along the West Coast. Native Americans apparently used it throughout its range. We only have one species in this area, the Black Haw Viburnum, and it makes good arrows though it is difficult to find a straight shoot which is long enough. There are other species, though, one of which is known as arrow-wood, which grows in the eastern part of the country. This species would probably yield much longer shoots and be easier to use.

Wild rose was another wood preferred for arrows by the Native Americans, as it was used by many tribes, both east and west. Because it does not grow on the Southern Plains, craftsmen there did not have the wild rose as a choice for their raw materials.

In the Western mountains and Great Basin chokecherry and serviceberry were made into arrows. Chokecherry especially was utilized since it was hard and stayed reasonably straight. People on the Northern Plains used chokecherry to some extent, too. Serviceberry arrowshafts a couple of thousand years old have been found in caves in Nevada and Utah.

On the West Coast, witch hazel was used a great deal for arrows. At least, it was one of the favorites of Ishi, the California Indian who came out of the wilderness in 1911. He made many arrows from witch hazel, and they illustrate beautiful, painstaking work. In his expert analysis witch hazel made good arrows, so we should defer to his opinion and be willing to use it, too.

The Northwest Coast Indians made arrows from small shoots like all the other tribes. But they also made arrowshafts much like modern ones are made, from a large cedar block that had long splinters split from it. The straight splinters were smoothed and rounded into excellent shafts.

There is another widespread plant that makes superior arrows, although it is not, strictly speaking, traditional. It is the Salt Cedar, or Tamarisk, which was introduced by the Europeans. Because of its late appearance, Native Americans were never able to utilize it. Salt Cedar makes outstanding shafts, though, so it's one you should be aware of. The wood is only medium hard, but its best quality is that it straightens easily and stays straight.

The willow seems like a natural for making arrows. It has small, straight shoots, grows everywhere, and everyone recognizes it. I've had miserable luck with it, though, because it's very soft and warps repeatedly, no matter how much it's straightened. Willow is definitely a last resort for arrows, since there are other, far better, traditional woods that should be available.

CUTTING AND SEASONING

Regardless of the type of wood you decide on, the techniques for cutting and seasoning the shaft will remain the same.

First of all, the wood should be cut in winter. The sap is down and the shafts will not split as badly during the drying process. Winter cut wood will experience some splitting, but nothing like wood cut in spring or summer. Wood cut when it's full of sap will split on the ends with the cracks sometimes travelling a foot or more from each end. The cracks will be 1/16" wide, or wider, and will render the shaft useless.

Another reason to cut shafts in the winter is that straight shoots are easier to see when the leaves have fallen. The choice shafts usually come from thickets where growth is crowded and plants have to grow quickly to compete for sunlight. In the summer these thickets will be opaque with leaves and the shoots growing within will be all but invisible.

The best dogwood thickets are found under larger trees which shade the plants and promote straighter growth. This is true of most other arrow woods as well, so if your chosen wood will grow in the shade of bigger trees, that is the place to start looking.

The shafts should be cut at least 6" longer than the finished arrow length. You'll want shafts about the size of your little finger, or a bit larger. They should be as straight as possible and free from any knots or other deformities. Any slight bends or crooked places in the shaft should be gradual, as these are not hard to take out later. A sharply angled bend or kink will disqualify a shaft, however, because the wood will never stay straight.

Be selective when cutting shafts. No shoots will be perfect, but care taken in their selection will results in much better arrows. Even if you're choosy when cutting the shafts, at the beginning there will probably be a high percentage of waste. Drying cracks, unseen deformities, and damage during the arrowmaking process can ruin quite a few shafts. When you first start, I suggest you cut at least twice as many shafts as you think you'll need. A reduction in waste will occur as you gain experience, but I still reject or ruin between 10% and 20% of all the shafts I start with.

When the shafts are cut, lash them into bundles of 10 or 20. Work each of these bundles through the entire arrowmaking process, when one step is finished the shafts are tied back into the same bundle. Leave the bark on during this initial drying process. If you wish, you can heat the shafts over coals or in the propane grill, bark and all, and give them a preliminary straightening before they are tied into bundles. As the lashing is pulled tight around the wood, the shafts should be arranged so they lay straight and evenly within the bundle. Keep the wood lashed together in a bunch for four to eight weeks.

SHAPING AND SIZING

Next, remove the bark from the shafts with a pocket knife, then the sizing begins. For this task I've come to prefer a small adjustable carpenter's plane, which is set very fine to take off only a small amount of wood at a time. The shaft should be straightened as much as possible before the shaping begins, so the plane will take wood from every surface and not just the outside of the bends. The plane will help straighten the shaft by taking off the high places, but it is desirable for the shaft to be reasonably straight when you start planning. Be sure to turn the shaft every time wood is taken off so the shaft will remain round and won't have a flat spot. Reduce the shaft's diameter until it is close to the finished size desired. Don't take off too much, just get close, since we're only roughing them in. The plane will take off any high spots on

Reducing the shaft with a carpenter's plane set very fine.

the wood, leaving an even shaft with no humps or valleys. Flint tools can be used for this process, as well as all of the other steps for making arrows, and will yield just as good a finished product although much more slowly.

When the sizing has been completed, tie the shafts into their bundles, being careful to lay them straight and evenly as the cord is tightened. The shafts need to be put aside in a shady place, protected from moisture, for two months to six months to allow them to season. A much longer drying time won't hurt the shafts, but I normally like to work them to finished shape within six months. The denser arrow woods will eventually dry into diamond-like hardness (well, almost), and become very hard to reduce. A two to six month seasoning time works very well for the roughed in shafts.

When the seasoning is completed, the shafts are reduced to their finished diameter. This can be done with the plane, set very fine, or with a Sureform woodworking plane. This type of plane looks like a miniature cheese grater,

Arrow making tools, a Surform plane, an adjustable carpenters plane, and a sizing tool.

Dogwood shafts in various stages of reduction. Top to bottom; raw shafts, shafts with preliminary sizing and straightening, finished shafts.

When cutting off a shaft, cut all the way around it, like this, so the shaft won't split.

and only takes off small amounts of wood at a time. As its shape is long and flat, it only takes wood from the high spots and yields an even shaft. Before beginning this step you'll want to cut off the arrows to within a couple of inches of their finished length. The extra length may allow you to cut off flaws, such as cracks in the ends or large knots.

To reduce the shafts, you'll need an arrow sizing tool, which is nothing more than a piece of wood or bone with a hole drilled through it the size of the finished shaft. My short 24" arrows are 9/32" diameter while the longer 28" ones are 5/16". Many of these original sizing tools are labeled as "arrow straighteners" and "arrow wrenches" in museums and archery books. Some of them may have been used to pry the crooks out of shafts, but in my opinion, any shaft that is so crooked or has such angular bends as to require an arrow wrench is worthless as an arrowshaft, anyway. The only time I've ever had need of an "arrow wrench" was to take out a bend right on the end of a shaft (a 7/16" boxend arrow wrench was my choice). I've had to use it only rarely, though, since it's much better to take off such a bend when cutting the shaft down close to the finished length. In any case, I believe most of the so-called arrow wrenches are mislabeled and were instead used to size the shafts and make them uniform.

The arrow sizer was used by starting the shaft through the hole, usually on the "point" end. A word about which end of the shaft should receive the point. Some Native Americans put the point on the "upper" end of the shaft while others placed it on the end that grew closest to the ground. I prefer placing the point on the upper end, because any knots where small branches grew will normally be located there, where they grew closest to the sunlight. It's better to have these knots on the bare shaft by the point, since any warpage that may occur around the knots will be easier to straighten in that area.

Sizing the shaft.

Several styles of Plains nocks.

Once the feathers are attached, it is very difficult to straighten a crooked shaft under them. When I peel the bark off of my shafts, I use a pencil to mark across the butt end so the marks won't be removed by subsequent scraping. Without the marks, it is sometimes difficult to tell which end is which after the shafts have been sized.

The point end of the shaft, whichever end you choose to use, will often have to be reduced in diameter before it will start into the sizer. When the shaft is worked down small enough to start into the hole, push the sizing tool up on the shaft as far as it will go. Remove the tool and notice that it has left a mark on the shaft. Work from that mark towards the large end of the shaft with one of the planes. When the shaft has been reduced further up its length, again run the sizing tool up on the shaft as far as it will go. This time, the tool should slide a little further before being stopped by the excess diameter of the shaft. Repeat this operation until the sizer will slide from one end of the shaft to the other. Take this step carefully, the sizer should just clear the shaft and be snug along its entire length. You want to avoid an hourglass shaped shaft where the sizer is loose because too much wood has been removed. This sizing allows you to produce a shaft of uniform diameter and also to make all of your arrows exactly the same size.

You may be making Plains-style arrows with a raised nock that is a larger diameter than the shaft. This was originally done in one of two ways. Use the arrow sizer and the plane until you get within about two or three inches of the nock. Reduce the remaining shaft with a fine woodrasp, while continuing to use the sizer, until you get within 1/4" to 3/8" of the end of the arrow. The extra wood remaining around the end will become the raised nock. This can also be done on the point end to make wooden blunts. Another way the larger

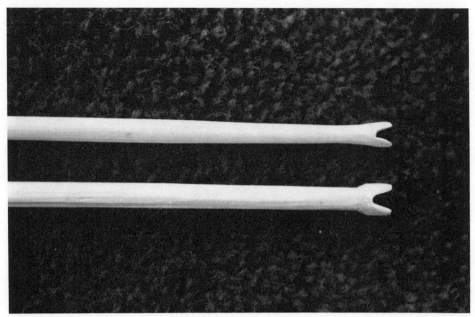

Two methods of making a raised nock for Plains-style arrows. These raised nocks give a better grip with a pinch-type release.

nock was traditionally made was to size the entire shaft, then remove wood from the shaft for several inches in front of the nock to make the nock larger in proportion. The reduced area was tapered into the nock as well as the rest of the shaft. This portion was considerably smaller than the remainder of the shaft, though the feathers mostly covered it up.

After the shaft is sized, and the nock shaped if you're making Plains-style arrows, the wood should be sanded. I like to use 220 or 320 grit sandpaper at this stage. The high spots and scraper marks should be sanded down, but don't get carried away and wind up with a shaft half the diameter that you wanted. One alternative is to roll the sandpaper snugly around the shaft and secure it with a rubber band. By running this tube of sandpaper up and down the shaft, any ridges or bumps disappear. One tube will last for many shafts and ensure that they're all the same. Often seen in museums are sets of sandstone shaft smoothers with a groove down their length, and these accomplish the same task. The smoothers are run up and down the shaft and the flat, abrasive sandstone takes down any high places while sanding the shaft.

The sized arrow shafts can be put back into bundles at this point, and left until they are ready for the finishing steps. Normally, if I don't complete the shafts immediately, I'll try to straighten and finish them within a month or so after they are sized.

TO GROOVE OR NOT TO GROOVE

When I first started making arrows, I wanted them to look as traditional as possible. I would completely finish an arrow, having straightened it with heat and polished it smooth, then run grooves down the length of the shaft, as the Native Americans of the plains and West Coast usually did. Having read that the grooves somehow relieved stresses in the wood, or represented lightning, or were "blood grooves," or were "ceremonial" in nature (translated: nobody had a clue what they were for), I always applied the grooves for appearances. But from the start I suspected they had to have some practical application, since the Native Americans were long-time masters at this craft and wouldn't have gone to that much trouble without a good reason.

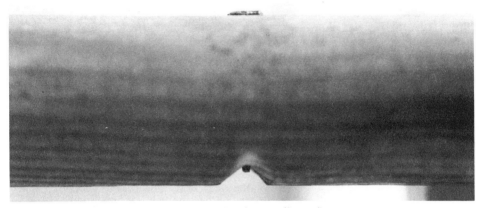

The grooving tool showing notch in the wood and protruding nail.

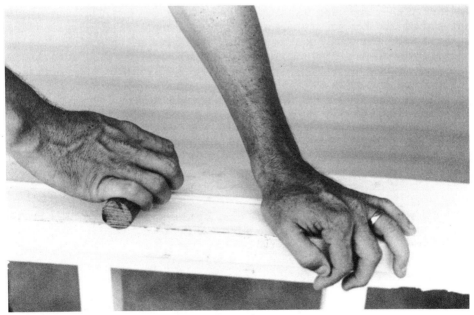

Using the grooving tool with the shaft on a flat surface.

After making a few hundred arrows, one time I varied the procedure. Instead of putting the grooves in after heating and straightening and polishing, I grooved the shafts as soon as they were sized. Then I applied grease and heated them in the propane grill to begin the final straightening process, which usually took several days. When I checked the shafts the next day, they had magically stayed straight, much straighter than ever before. I knew I had accidentally rediscovered what the Native American arrowmakers had known all along, that the grooves keep the shaft straight when the grooves are heated. I wasn't sure at first why it worked, I just knew that grooving the shafts before the heating process yielded much straighter arrows.

Over time, I came to understand why the grooves function, and why so many old-time arrowmakers used to groove their arrows. As usual, the explanation was wonderfully simple. When wood is heated it is hardened, so when the grooved arrows had heat applied to them the ridges down either side of the groove were exposed to more heat and thus became harder than the rest of the wood. These hardened ridges, six all together when using three grooves, acted as "stiffeners" and helped prevent the shaft from warping. How this technique was originally discovered and used, I haven't a hint, but some Indian Einstein has passed along a way for us to make much better arrows.

The original arrows sometimes had two but usually three grooves down their length. I've come to prefer three straight grooves, from one end of the shaft to the other, although some originals had undulating grooves down them. A variation on this was a groove which started straight on the feather end, then had four or five squiggles in front of the fletching, after which the groove continued straight to the point end. Some arrows had one or two straight grooves with the remaining grooves being crooked. I've even seen a few arrows that had the grooves running around and around the shaft, like a barber's pole. There isn't much difference, that I can tell, in straight grooves, wiggly grooves, or a combination, since they all serve the same purpose. So take your choice.

The actual groover is a simple affair, just a notch with a protrusion that can all be made from flint, bone, or metal. The arrow is laid on a flat surface, then the notch of the groover placed over the shaft and, with downward pressure applied, the groover is dragged from one end of the shaft to the other. The notch holds the tool in place on the shaft with the protrusion scraping out the groove. If the first groove is not deep enough, the process can be repeated, since the original groove will tend to guide the groover down the same path.

Not all original arrows were grooved, but many on the West Coast were along with the vast majority of Plains arrows. This technique can be employed with any type or style of wooden arrow so it's one you should probably be using since the finished product is much improved.

STRAIGHTENING

Once the arrow shafts are sized, have had the preliminary sanding done, and are grooved, they will be regular and smooth although not straight. They will still have bends in them but the bends should be gradual. Any shaft with a sharp, angular bend will be very hard to straighten and will probably not stay straight. It should be culled at this point, if it hasn't been already.

The original ten or twenty shafts in a bundle have probably been reduced in number as the arrowmaking has proceeded. Cracks, rotten knots, sharp bends, insect damage, or cutting too small or crooked a shaft in the first place are all reasons to have rejected a shaft by this stage. You should also reject any with splinters or cracks as they would be dangerous to shoot. I like to work the shafts through the straightening process in even numbers of ten or twenty, so some of the bundles that have been reduced by attrition may need to be combined at this point.

The arrow shafts are bent and straightened much as the bow wood was bent, with grease and heat. The grease helps the heat to penetrate and will aid in preventing the wood from becoming scorched. The grease can be from many sources, and although I prefer shortening, the oil can be bacon grease, deer fat, cooking oil, bear grease, or just about any other kind of animal or vegetable oil. The heat can be generated by the coals of a campfire, and I have spent many winter evenings straightening arrows by the fireplace. The simplest and easiest, however, is the all-purpose propane grill, as it's quick to heat up, the heat is even, and the temperature can be precisely controlled.

The grill should be set on low to medium heat, which can be adjusted as needed. The shafts are coated with the grease and placed in the hot grill one at a time. After twenty or thirty seconds the shaft should be turned half a 'turn, so it won't become scorched on one side and the heat will penetrate more evenly. Usually, a minute or so is enough heating time, although this will vary considerably according to the amount of heat, the type of shaft, and the diameter of the wood. The wood should never be allowed to get scorched, but must reach a high enough temperature to render the shaft very flexible.

When the shaft is first removed from the heat, it will be far too hot to handle with bare hands, so a couple of pot holders can be used for protection. Hold the end of the shaft up to one eye and turn it, any bends will be obvious. You can start bending the shaft with the potholders to begin taking out the most apparent crooks. When the shaft cools enough so that you can handle it with bare hands, it will be easier to see and work out any bends. Be sure to reverse the shaft while you're working on it, sometimes a bend difficult to see from one end will be clearly evident from the other. Some shafts can be straightened in just a few seconds, while others will take several minutes of bending, rebending, and re-rebending. Don't give up until the shaft is completely straight. Once the shaft is perfectly straight, lay it aside on a flat surface to cool, then place another shaft in the grill.

After the shafts have all been through the straightening process, they should be set aside overnight on a flat surface. They can be reexamined the next day and any minor crooks taken out. Be sure to check the shafts from both ends to detect the slightest bend. One or two shafts out of ten may have warped badly enough to require reheating and restraightening; this is to be expected and will not hurt the shaft. After a shaft has been reheated and restraightened two or three times and will still not stay reasonably straight it should be rejected, since it will never make a good arrow. And you only thought I was kidding about wasting up to half of the shafts by the time we got to this point.

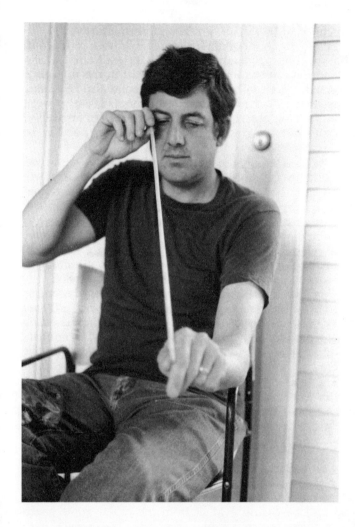

Looking down the shaft while turning it makes any bends readily apparent.

I prefer to straighten arrows by hand, but some of the original arrowmakers, and a few Native Americans today, straighten their arrows by holding a crooked place in their mouth and pulling down on both ends of the shaft. A significant number of arrows in museums, and especially arrows from the Southern Plains, still exhibit teeth marks in the wood from when the shaft was straightened. I once had a museum curator give me a ten minute lecture about indentations left in an original Kiowa arrow by the famous "arrow wrench." Since he undoubtedly had nine degrees in Anthropology, I refrained from mentioning that the arrow wrench was once attached to someone's jaw-bone. To be fair, on another occasion, in a different museum, a curator was delighted when I told her that the arrowmakers' teeth had caused the tiny indentations that could be seen on an arrowshaft when it was held up to the light.

FINISHING

Now that the arrows have been straightened, and have remained straight, they can be sanded down to the final finish. You may need to wipe off the shafts to remove any leftover grease from the heating process, because the grease will clog the sandpaper. Go over the shafts with 400 grit sandpaper and then with 600 grit. I like to only use fine grit sandpaper after the shafts are grooved because it removes very little of the hardened ridges that make the grooves work.

The 600 grit sandpaper will polish the shafts, but a further, even more lustrous polish can be applied by burnishing the arrows, much like we did to the bow earlier. This is done by rubbing and compressing the surface of the wood with a hard object, such as a bone tool or even a small glass bottle. This burnishing will yield a beautiful mirror-like finish.

NOCKS

The nocks, or notches for the bowstring, can be cut into the arrows before or after the final sanding step. The nocks are started into the shaft with a hacksaw, cutting down the exact center of the arrow until the required depth is reached. This depth will vary, depending on the style of arrow you are making. Clean out the nock and widen it with a very sharp knife (a razor blade knife works well for this), until the desired shape and width are attained. The bottom of the nock can then be rounded and smoothed with a small round file. Carefully use the knife to trim off and slightly round any sharp edges left from cutting the nock, this will protect your bowstring from possible damage.

Unless you plan to crest the shafts, or paint them (refer to the next section), they can now be finished with a thin coating of oil. Rub the oil well into the shafts, wipe off any excess, check them one last time for straightness, and the arrowshafts are completed. They can be tied into bundles and stored indefinitely, until you are ready to apply feathers and points.

CRESTING

Most original arrowshafts were painted before the feathers were applied. This painting was done to some degree for decoration, but, more practically, to identify arrows and signify their ownership. When everyone in a camp had a quiver full of arrows, and was always working on more, it would not be hard to get arrows mixed up without some distinctive markings. Also, after a communal hunt, the ownership marks on an arrow would designate who had killed which animals, or would settle a dispute if more than one man's arrow was found in an animal by showing which arrow had caused the fatal wound. After a battle, where there may have been hundreds of arrows lying about, the markings of the owner would show who had killed which enemy. And, when a hunt or a battle were finished, the distinctively marked arrows which missed their mark could be found and claimed by their owner. Except, as was usually the case after a big fight, some men would forego looking for trophies and would begin picking up the arrows. Arrows picked up in this manner generally belonged to the man who found them, so he could salvage an armload of arrows and save a couple of months of work.

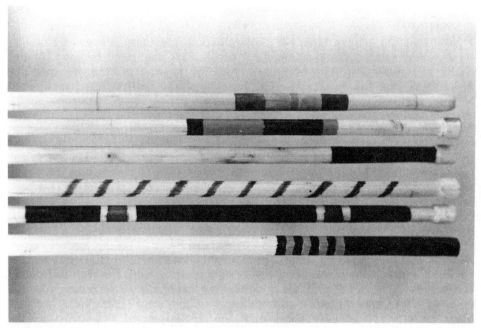

Painted designs. Top to bottom; three colors (which was somewhat unusual), two colors, a single color (usually red or black), barber pole design with one color, design that will cover the entire shaft under the feathers, and a West Coast design with small bands.

Anyway, most of the arrows were marked in some way, usually by painting the shaft. The paints were normally powdered earth pigments mixed with a medium, such as the sticky juice from a prickly pear cactus pad, to seal and help waterproof the paint. The primary colors used were red, brown, yellow, black, blue, and sometimes green. A good modern substitute for these earth paints is acrylic paint, which comes in a tube from artists' supply stores. The acrylic paint can be purchased in traditional colors, or the colors can be toned down by adding a bit of brown paint to the mixture. Acrylic paint is water soluble, and can be thinned with water enough to make it look like the original colors. Even though the paint is water based, once it is dry it will not wash off, which is a problem associated with earth paints.

The painting was normally done where the feathers would be placed, so the design could be seen between the feathers. In many cases, only one color of paint was used and applied in a single band, an inch or two wide, around the arrow. Usually two colors were used to form a design but sometimes three colors were employed. On rare occasion, an entire shaft was painted one color, usually red, or the grooves in an arrow were painted.

In the late 1800's commercial paints were sometimes employed for arrows. The colors became brighter and more varied. One of the most striking and distinctive of these was on the Southern Plains where laundry blueing, normally for whitening clothes in the wash, was used to stain their arrows a dark bluish-green. This same blueing can still sometimes be found in old-time hardware stores.

Arrows were occasionally painted on the point end, too. On the West Coast the arrows might be stained red or black for two or three inches behind the point. The hardwood foreshaft on Southwestern and West Coast reed arrows was sometimes painted completely in red or black. I have examined a couple of sets of arrows from the Comanches with the first three inches of the shaft painted with laundry blueing, sinew wrapping and all.

It's a good idea to test the colors and designs you plan to use on a broken or discarded shaft. Once you've decided on the markings, measure all of the shafts and make a small mark with a pencil where each of the designs will go. This will keep the painting symmetrical and uniform.

When the paint is totally dry, usually overnight, the shafts should be oiled, straightened one more time, and then bundled until you are ready to complete the arrow.

REED ARROWSHAFTS

Arrows made from reeds were used extensively across the country, wherever the reeds where available. Reed arrows were sometimes used almost exclusively by a particular group, such as by the Cherokees in the East, but were more often employed along with hardwood arrowshafts. The Native Americans of the West Coast made most of their arrows from hardwood, for instance, but used reed for perhaps a quarter to a third of their arrows. About half of the Apache arrows that I have examined in museums were made from reed. About the only place where reed arrowshafts were not used extensively was on the Great Plains, where they didn't normally grow, although I have seen one set of Comanche arrows that were made from reed.

The Indian people utilized reed shafts a great deal because it made such good arrows. They were light, stiff, and easy to obtain. The light, hollow shafts will fly much faster than a heavy hardwood arrow, which makes them easier to shoot accurately since they don't drop as much in flight. I try to avoid being overly scientific, but was recently able to shoot some reed arrows through a chronograph, and the results were mildly surprising. With a 60# Osage Orange bow, I first shot a heavy dogwood arrow, with a steel point, at a very reasonable 165 feet per second. I shot a reed arrow next, with the same bow, and it clocked 198 feet per second, which is quite unreasonable. In fact, I had to repeat the performance several times because the longbow and recurve shooters standing around couldn't believe it.

THE SHAFT

A couple of different types of reed were used to make arrows. The most prominent and widespread was Phragmites Reed, which grows from the West Coast to the Rocky Mountains, and from the Gulf Coast to the Midwest. A reed known as "switch cane" was used in the Southeast.

The reed for arrows should be cut in the fall when the shafts have matured completely, but before they dry out and are exposed to too much cold weather. A shaft should be cut at least twelve and preferably eighteen inches longer than is needed for the finished arrow. Even more than with hardwood arrows, you need to be selective when cutting reed shafts. The reeds can be straightened to some degree, but should be nearly straight when cut, with no angular bends where the joints of the cane grew. Be aware that the reeds taper in diameter, so the shafts should be 3/8" to 7/16" on the large end. The completed arrow will be about 3/8" on the big end, and because the reed cannot be reduced in diameter, the extra foot or more that was cut will allow you to place the arrow in the reed where it will be the proper size. Again, if you're a beginning arrowmaker, you'll probably want to cut twice as many shafts as needed for finished arrows.

When the shafts are all cut, the leaves should be trimmed off. The shafts are then cut to a uniform length, though still much longer than needed for the finished arrow. The arrows are not bundled as were the hardwood shafts but spread out in the shade to dry.

The reed arrowshafts may be straightened and worked immediately, but I prefer to give them a drying time of from two to six weeks. After this drying period, treat the shafts with grease and heat in the same manner as wooden shafts in order to straighten them. The reed will be much stiffer than the wooden shafts, however, and won't tolerate as much bending. When they are bent too far they suddenly give way and are crushed on the inside of the curve. If the reed shafts were reasonably straight to begin with, though, and have no abrupt angular bends, they can be straightened with the judicious use of grease and heat.

After all of the shafts have been straightened (or culled), you need to make an arrowshaft that will be used as a pattern for the others. Choose one that will be 3/8" on the large end, and cut it off 1¼" in front of a joint. Measure the length of the finished arrow towards the small end and cut off the shaft. Be aware that a reed arrow is not drawn to the point, but is only drawn back for the length of the reed. Cut the first reed accordingly. Use this first arrow to find the proper diameter within the longer remaining shafts and cut them to length. Remember to cut the large end on all of the shafts 1¼" in front of a joint. The added strength of the joint area will help withstand the stresses when the arrow hits a target.

The excess material around all of the joints in each shaft requires trimming and smoothing. The large end of the shaft will be the front of the arrow, so the trimming should be done towards the butt, or smaller, end. This lets the

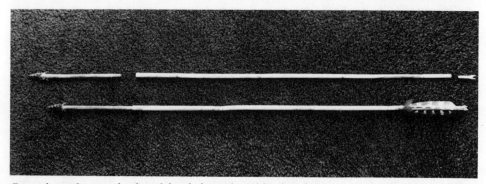

Parts of a reed arrow, hardwood foreshaft, reed, and hardwood nock.

arrow slide smoothly across the hand when shooting, with no splinters or rough places that can snag. When the shafts are smoothed, they should be checked for straightness. Any crooks can again be worked with heat if necessary.

The shafts are now put into bundles of ten or twenty and wrapped with cord, but you must be careful not to get the cord too tight or the shafts may be crushed. They can be stored this way until you are ready to finish them.

Method for making the front of a reed shaft smaller so as to fit the foreshaft. A narrow notch is cut on both sides of the reed.

The sinew wrapping squeezes the notch together and makes the shaft diameter smaller.

FORESHAFT

Since a reed arrow is not sturdy enough to withstand the stress that an arrowhead places on it when hitting a target, a hardwood "foreshaft" with the point attached is fitted into the front of the arrow. The foreshaft is normally 3" to 7" long, depending on the type of arrow you are making. These foreshafts are a good way to make use of the broken or culled hardwood shafts that have already been worked down to size.

The foreshaft should be about 1/4" to 5/16" in diameter. If it is too big to fit in the socket on the front of the reed arrowshaft, one end can be tapered down until it is a snug fit. If the foreshaft is a bit too small and loose, the end of the reed can be narrowly notched so the diameter of the reed will be slightly reduced when it is wrapped with sinew.

The leading edge of the reed (again, the large end), should be tapered evenly all the way around so it will blend into the foreshaft. Then wrap the reed with flat loin sinew back to the first joint. This supports the shaft and keeps it from breaking.

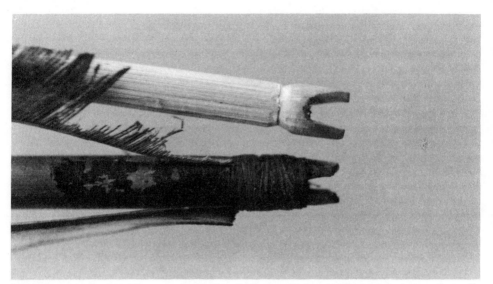

Two types of nocks on reed arrows. A hardwood plug can be inserted for a nock, top, or the nock can be cut directly into the reed as on this original Apache arrow (author's collection).

The hardwood nock glued into the reed makes a much sturdier arrow.

NOCKS

The nock to accept the string can be cut directly into the shaft. The string would probably split the reed when an arrow is released except for the sinew wrapping on the upper end of the fletching which helps strengthen the shaft. The nocks cut directly in a reed shaft were fairly shallow, about 1/4" deep. The sharp corners on the back of the shaft were rounded to prevent damage to the bowstring. The vast majority of Indians cut the nocks directly into an arrow in this way.

A much sturdier and more durable method sometimes employed was to make a small hardwood nock whose end could be inserted into the reed shaft. The nock was glued into place, then wrapped with sinew when the fletching was applied. To make a long-lasting set of hunting arrows, I would recommend using this hardwood nock.

FLETCHING

In theory, the purpose of feathers on an arrow is to create enough drag to keep the backend of the arrow behind the front end. How well and evenly this drag is created, however, will largely determine how straight the arrow will fly.

TYPES OF FEATHERS

Feathers from virtually every type of bird were used at one time or another for making arrows. The Native American arrowmakers did come to have a few preferences when there was a choice. They used mainly feathers from large birds. I have seen old arrows with fletchings from bald and golden eagle, at least ten different types of hawks, two types of buzzards, turkey, crane, goose, and owl. When large feathers were not available, feathers from smaller birds, such as crow, roadrunner, or grouse would be used.

In general, Indians would use predatory bird feathers when they were available, though this probably stems as much from "medicine" as from a strictly practical application. One exception is owl feathers. The only two sets of arrows I have ever seen with owl fletching came from the Northern Plains. Many Indian tribes did not care for owls, they reminded them of ghosts flying about hooting in the darkness, but there was a functional drawback, as well. Owl feathers are so soft, to allow them to fly silently, that they are very easily crushed and distorted. As a result, they are not desirable for fletching.

The best feathers come from a wild turkey. First of all, they are legal to possess and use, which eagle, hawk, and buzzard feathers are decidedly not. Legalities aside, turkey feathers are superior to any others because they are thicker and less prone to damage or distortion. The wing feathers in particular are sturdy and easy to prepare.

Which brings us to another consideration; using wing or tail feathers? Either is good, and the Native American arrowmakers used wings and tails about equally. Ideally, the feathers on a particular arrow would come from the same side of the bird; three feathers from the right wing, three feathers from the left, or three feathers from either side of the tail. Usually, feathers from the

Turkey wing feathers, three lefts and three rights.

Turkey tail feathers, three lefts and three rights.

same bird were used, although it was common to see arrows with feathers from three different species of hawks, for instance. The same standard about three rights or three lefts still applied, though, so the arrow would fly well. But rarely, probably because of a shortage of feathers, rights and lefts would be mixed together, or, just as detrimental to arrow flight, wing and tail feathers would be mixed.

PREPARING FEATHERS

Wing and tail feathers are prepared in the same manner, with the exception of turkey wings, which we'll cover later. The feathers are worked through the process three at a time and are kept together until placed on the arrow.

An individual feather is placed on a flat surface, then the spine scraped with a sharp blade or flint chip. This is done to make the feather thin so it will lay flatter on the arrow. It is easier to thin the spine while the feather is intact than after it is split. The inside bend of the feather will be thicker and require more scraping to thin, but the outside of the feather should be scraped, too, especially toward the front where it is thickest. Scrape the spine of the feather until it gets down fairly close to the vanes. The spine should be evenly scraped, with no gouges or humps. You will want to scrape the feather less the further toward the tip you go.

Next, split the feather by sharply rapping the spine, front and back, along its length with the back of a pocket knife. This cracks the feather along a natural groove. A sharp blade is used to split the spine, starting at the large end. Where the spine becomes very slender, within two or three inches of the end of the feather, you'll want to cut across it towards the narrow side of the feather. The wide side of the feather is used, and you don't want to risk a slip and cut across the spine the wrong way.

Tail feather split and trimmed.

When the wide side of the feather is separated, the spine can be trimmed and evened with scissors or by careful scraping. The feather is then shaped by cutting off vanes right along the spine, starting at the back. The vanes are trimmed for two or three inches, depending on how much feather you have to work with. Measure from the back of the remaining vane the length that the finished feather will be. Separate the vanes at that point and peel off the excess vanes towards the front of the feather. The feather is now roughed in and ready to place on the arrow.

Turkey wing feathers can be worked much more quickly by "stripping" the feathers than by splitting them. Tail feathers can't be done this way and I've never found another type of birds' wing feathers that can be consistently stripped. This is another reason why turkey wing fletching is so desirable. The stripping is done by holding the tip of the feather in the left hand, with the wide side of the feather to the right. With your right hand, at the end of the feather and right next to the fingers of the left hand, grasp the vanes by the spine and pull to the right and downward. You will probably destroy a few feathers until you get the feel of what should happen, but when done properly, the vanes, and their thin connected bases, can be cleanly stripped clear of the spine of the feather in about ten seconds. The vanes are then trimmed from both ends as described earlier, and the feather is ready.

Stripping a turkey wing feather from the small end.

APPLYING FEATHERS WITH GLUE

Most of the Native American arrowmakers used glue as well as sinew wrapping to attach their feathers. When the entire spine of the feather is glued down, instead of just being wrapped on either end, it helps protect the feather from damage and keeps it from pulling away from the shaft in the middle. Good arrows can be made without glue, but I recommend using it if possible.

To attach the feathers, first determine where they will be placed on the arrow. The back of the fletching should be 1/2" to 1" in front of the nock. I like to place them 1" forward so my fingers don't touch the feathers when holding an arrow on the bowstring. Place one of the prepared feathers on the shaft and determine where the back of the feather will go. Make a pencil mark on the shaft at the front edge of the remaining vanes of the feather. Just in front of this mark is where the sinew wrapping will begin. If you're using a reed arrowshaft, it's a good idea to rough up the slick shaft with sandpaper at this point, so the glue will have something to hold onto and the feathers won't come loose.

The sinew for attaching feathers comes from the back of an animal and is very long and thin. Narrow threads can be split from the main piece and moistened to make them flexible. The thin threads can be soaked in a pan of water to prepare them, but a superior method is the one the Native Americans used, to gently chew the individual pieces of sinew. The chewing, along with the moistening of the saliva, renders the sinew usable much more quickly than mere soaking and makes the sinew softer and easier to apply smoothly. A Native American arrowmaker once told me that he always swallowed any small pieces of sinew that came loose from the main piece. He said when you start swallowing the sinew instead of spitting it out, you have made an arrowmaker. Of course, I immediately started swallowing the remnants of sinew, but it seems like I had to make another few hundred arrows before there was much improvement.

When you start trying to attach three feathers to a wooden shaft with a thread of sinew, logic would tell you that you need five hands. Sometimes you do. You can turn your entire body into a weapon, though, by holding the shaft in the crook behind a knee and using your teeth to hold the end of the sinew. This leaves both hands free to arrange the feathers.

With the arrowshaft held by your leg, begin by wrapping one end of the sinew just in front of the mark made on the shaft. Make a couple of turns around the shaft to lock the end of the sinew down. Place the end of the sinew between your teeth to hold it snugly and put the first feather on the shaft. The leading edge of the feather vanes should lie right on the pencil mark. Turn the arrow and feather until the sinew, still held by your teeth, wraps over the trimmed spine of the feather to hold it in place. Put the next feather on the arrow and turn the shaft until the sinew holds it. Do the same with the last feather. Don't worry too much at this point about having the feathers exactly spaced on the shaft, just have them spread out. It will take some practice, but you should soon be able to place all three feathers on the arrow with one complete turn of the shaft.

A word about the "cock" feather, or the feather that in modern times is placed at right angles to the nock. This is done so that the feathers can clear

Holding the arrow shaft behind one knee with the end of the sinew in the mouth leaves both hands free.

the bow more easily when an arrow is released. I'm not sure if Indian arrow-makers were all aware of the advantages of a cock feather, but some certainly were. There is a set of Sioux arrows in the storage area of the Field Museum, in Chicago, that have two buzzard feathers with one hawk feather. The hawk feather is lined up on all of the arrows as a cock feather, so it would be quicker to identify and place an arrow on the string properly. Not all Indian arrows had a feather lined up at right angles to the nock, but many did, and since it's advantageous to arrow flight I suggest you do the same. The first feather you place on the shaft should be the cock feather. Place it at right angles to the nock and the other feathers will be lined up on it.

After the three feathers are initially set on the arrow, make two or three turns of the shaft, while holding tension on the sinew. Rather than wrap the sinew around the arrow, the arrow is turned to roll up the sinew towards the front of the shaft. When the feathers are secured with several wraps they need to be evenly spaced. Look at the arrow from the nock end and you can see which ones should be moved. Don't move the cock feather, move the other two in relation to it. The feathers will be easy to move since the sinew is still moist and there are only a couple of wraps of sinew around them. Make sure to hold the end of the sinew tightly so the feathers don't shift or fall off. Move

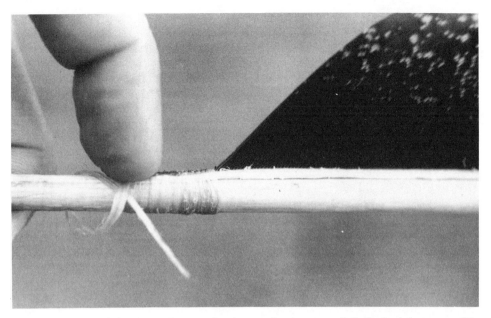

Tying off the end of the sinew. Be sure the sinew end points toward the back of the arrow, this prevents any protrusions that can snag the bow hand when an arrow is released.

the feathers until they are exactly spaced around the arrow, then continue turning the shaft to wrap the sinew evenly towards the front of the arrow.

As you get close to the end of the sinew, the leftover spine should be carefully trimmed. It should be tapered forward with a sharp blade. The sinew wrapping is continued to completely cover the leading edges of the feathers' spines. The wrapping on the front of the feather has to be carefully and smoothly done, with no protrusions, because the arrow is shot across the hand that holds the bow and any protrusions can cause a cut. When you get to the end of the sinew, simply tuck the sinew under itself and tighten the free end with pliers. Moisten the thumb and forefinger and hold them snugly on the sinew wrapping as you turn the arrow. This pressure, applied while the sinew is still soft and pliable, will smooth the sinew completely and help take out any rough spots.

The back of the feather now has to be secured. Begin right at the base of the nock with another piece of sinew and make a couple of wraps to secure it. Wrap the sinew around the tail of the cock feather first, then secure the ends of the other two and make three or four additional wraps. The tail of the feathers should now be spaced as the fronts were earlier. There are two ways to place the feathers. One is to line up the backs of the feathers exactly behind the fronts, where the feather lies straight down the shaft. Most Native American arrows were fletched with this method, and the natural twist of the feathers would give the arrow a modest spin when shot. The other way to place the feathers is to twist the rear of them about an eighth of a turn around the shaft in relation to the front. This gives the arrow more spin and makes it stabilize

Feathers attached with sinew at the front.

Back of the feathers tied down with sinew. Note the twist imparted to the feathers by the way they are arranged.

Back view of same arrow clearly shows twist. The twist makes the arrows spin and fly straighter.

more quickly in flight. Remember to twist the feather in the direction it naturally wants to go to expose the inside of the feather to the air.

Once the rear of the feathers are spaced evenly and placed in relation to the front of the feather, the tail of the feather, behind the nock, should be pulled to snug the feather against the shaft. Continue wrapping the sinew forward and pull the tail of each feather again. Don't pull hard enough to break the feather, but it should be snug and lie flat and even against the shaft. Continue wrapping the sinew to the base of the vanes. The sinew should then be tucked under itself and pulled tightly. The extra tail of the sinew can be cut off and the wrapping turned between the moistened fingers to smooth it.

Now is the time to glue down the feather with the liquid hide glue. Remember that while the liquid glue was unsuitable for backing bows because of the retarder in it, the very thin amount placed on arrows sets up within an hour or two. The liquid glue is handy because it's ready to use instantly, without having to heat up the glue pot, and tiny amounts can be used at a time.

To glue down the feathers, hold the arrow in the crook of your leg and squeeze out a drop of glue onto a toothpick. Push the vane of the feather over until the underside of the spine is exposed. Use the toothpick to apply an even coating of glue to the spine of the feather throughout its length. When the glue has been applied to a feather, pull steadily and firmly one last time on the tail to snug it down. Wipe off any extra glue that gets on the shaft or comes out from under the feather. After treating all three feathers in the same

Using a toothpick to apply hide glue to the underside of the feathers' spine.

way, trim off the excess tail behind the nock, then put the arrow aside for the glue and sinew to dry completely. When the arrow has dried, usually after a couple of hours, the sinew can be finished by cutting off any hard ends with fingernail clippers. The fletching is now complete, so you can refer to the section on trimming feathers and decoration.

APPLYING FEATHERS WITHOUT GLUE

Good arrows can be made without glue, but the problem encountered is that the feathers tend to pull away from the shaft between the sinew lashings on either end. The feathers raise up as a result of expansion and contraction that accompanies changes in temperature and relative humidity. The ends of the feathers move slightly under the sinew wrapping, and eventually the feathers no longer lie snugly against the shaft. There are several steps you can take, however, to keep this from happening or minimize its effect.

Many times a feather that is not glued down will raise up.

The back of a feather attached without glue is tied down like this.

The first thing that can be done is to lock down one end of the feather so it can't move. The feather will be attached differently than if glue were being used because this time the tail end of the feather is lashed down first. Place the "hook" on the end of the tail next to the nock and wrap it. Once all three feathers are attached and evenly positioned in this way, fold them forward and wrap the spines completely with sinew. This doubles the spine upon itself and prevents it from moving. There are a couple of variations on this as shown in the photos.

Once the back of the feather is secured, the front of the fletching is attached. One way to help prevent the feather from moving here is to put small grooves around the shaft where the sinew wrapping will go. The grooves give the sinew a better grip on the spine of the feather and helps keep it stationary. This method was commonly used on the West Coast.

Another method for attaching the back of a feather without glue.

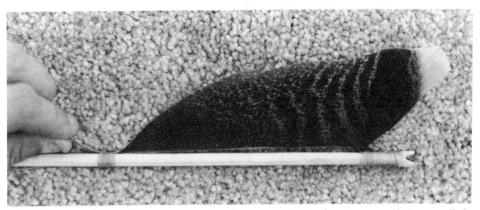

When the front of the feathers are arranged and secured with five or six wraps of sinew, pull the spine of the feather to tighten it against the shaft.

The front spine of the feathers can be tacked down with pitch glue if no hide glue is available. This adhesive is made by melting balls of pitch from the pine or cedar trees, then mixing a small amount of powdered charcoal into it so it won't be so brittle. When the front spines of the feathers have been wrapped several times with sinew and precisely arranged, the pitch glue can be daubed under the remaining spine. Pull the feathers snugly using the extra spine in front. The sinew is then wrapped forward across the rest of the spine along with the pitch. The front of the feathers are treated in the same manner with this method as they were for using glue. When you get close to the end of the sinew trim the excess spine at a taper and completely cover it with the remaining sinew. Remember to arrange the feathers carefully as they are being attached, by laying the feathers on straight or putting in a twist to make the arrow spin as discussed earlier. The use of pitch glue, along with the grooves around the shaft, was used by Native American arrowmakers and remains an effective way to make serviceable arrows when no hide glue is available.

Another alternative for attaching feathers with no glue was employed by Eastern Indians. The feathers are put on the shaft and snugged down as de-

Completed feather attached with no glue.

An Eastern-style fletch with no glue. The feather is secured at both ends with sinew then wrapped for its entire length with a sinew thread. Note feather decoration (in this case green) applied under front sinew after sinew is halfway wrapped.

An Eastern three feather fletch using whole feathers. With this method, as with all the others, be sure to use feathers from the same side of the bird.

End view of same arrow showing how feathers lay and the spin that they naturally give arrow.

scribed earlier for making arrows with glue. It helps to trim the feathers to their finished height at this point, they are secured and the trimming will make the rest of this technique much easier. After the feathers are trimmed, another long piece of moist sinew is started just before the front of the feather. This sinew winds around and around the arrow towards the back, and as it crosses each feather the vanes are separated to accommodate it. Since the feathers have already been trimmed it is easier to see where to separate the vanes. When the piece of sinew has been wound around the feather to the back, barber-pole fashion, secure it with a half hitch. The feathers are then smoothed back together over the sinew. This method makes a good fletching that will not come loose.

Another option for attaching feathers without glue consists of using the entire tail feather of a smaller bird, such as a crow or heron. The feathers are prepared by stripping away, on both sides of the spine, some of the vane at the leading edge of the feather. Otherwise, leave the feathers intact. Attach the bare spine with sinew at the front of the fletching as described for gluing feathers. The feathers are arranged exactly like any other three feather fletch, as shown in the photo from the nock end. The rear sinew wrapping goes over the entire feather, vane and all. This method makes an accurate fletch that won't raise up because an entire feather is used. The only drawback is that the small, relatively soft feathers are prone to becoming crushed if left in a quiver or laid flat.

A two feather fletch with whole feathers was used by the eastern Cherokees.

Cherokees in the eastern part of the country commonly used a two-feather fletch which utilized whole feathers, as well. The vanes are trimmed but the spine is left intact. With this two feather method, the feathers are placed on opposite sides of the arrow, parallel with the plane of the nock. The feathers are attached at the front, in an inverted position, then folded upon themselves as the feather is pulled back to the rear. The back of the feather is wrapped with sinew and the fletching pulled tight from there. As a result of the way the feathers were trimmed, the natural twist in them makes the arrow spin.

TRIMMING AND DECORATION

The feathers can be trimmed in different ways, depending on which regional style you are making. In general, a feather trimmed lower is less susceptible to damage or distortion, so I trim mine to about 1/2" tall. I like to square off the points of the feathers at the back, so the fingers don't touch the feathers and make noise while you're hunting. The feathers can also be trimmed purely for decoration or ownership marks. The notches cut in the edge of the feathers or the middle section of feather trimmed down to the spine are both old-time examples of this. Although trimming the feathers in this way added little to their accuracy, it is attractive and striking none the less.

When it comes to traditional decorations on arrows, I wrap a brightly colored bit of fluff under the sinew at the leading edge of each feather. The bright color makes it easier to see the arrow in flight and to see a shaft that has been lost. It may be my imagination, too, but it seems as if the arrows with fluffs stabilize quicker and shoot more accurately. The fluffs, in the old days, were usually white or natural colors, though I have seen them dyed red, blue, yellow, and green.

The back of these feathers have had the tips squared off so the fingers won't touch them when shooting.

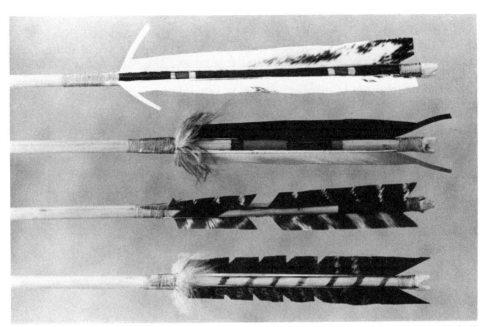

Decoration, top to bottom; leading vanes left long and the back of the feathers squared off, fluffs placed at leading edge of feathers and vanes left long at the back, vanes trimmed down to shaft in the middle of the feather, and notches cut into edge of feather along with fluffs placed at the front.

Sometimes brightly colored feathers instead of fluffs were attached to the front of the fletching under the sinew. I have seen Blue Jay, the red and yellow feathers from a Red-winged Black Bird, woodpecker, and the breast feathers from a meadowlark, among others, used for decoration on original arrows. These feathers were usually placed when the large fletching feathers were secured, but sometimes were not put on until the sinew wrapping was more than half done.

POINTS

BLUNTS

The purpose of our entire exercise of building bows, arrows, and strings has been to deliver a traditional point to a target. In the old days, a large proportion of the arrows had no point as such, but had blunt tips. Unless a group lived in an unusually game-rich area, like the Plains, a great deal of their efforts were spent on small game. So a blunt was adequate for the task and easy to make. In the 1930's, in a cave in the Gila River area of New Mexico, a cache of several thousand reed arrows was found. Less than a dozen of the arrows had stone points, the rest were hardwood blunts [5].

A blunt can be created in two ways. The shaft, or foreshaft in the case of a

---

5. *Hibben, American Antiquity (July, 1938)*

reed arrow, can be sharpened so it will penetrate then hardened over coals. This is the way most of the arrows found in the cave were done. Another way is to leave a bulb of wood on the front of the arrow. The bulb, up to 3/4" diameter, can be flattened on the front or rounded. This method prevents the arrow from penetrating but instead delivers tremendous shocking power to small game. Both types of blunts were found throughout the country.

Top to bottom; flint from Edwards County, Texas, steel, buffalo bone, and obsidian from Glass Butte, Oregon.

STONE

Before the advent of steel, virtually all big-game arrows were tipped with obsidian or flint. Man has kept himself fed on this continent for the last fifteen thousand years with flint spears, dart points, and later arrowheads, so they are clearly effective. In my experience, flint points are just as good as steel when it comes to penetration and sharpness. The drawback to flint is that it is brittle, if you miss a target or hit a bone the point is destroyed. They are also time-consuming to make, what with quarrying the stone, reducing it to blanks with a hammerstone, heat treating, the actual pressure flaking with a deer

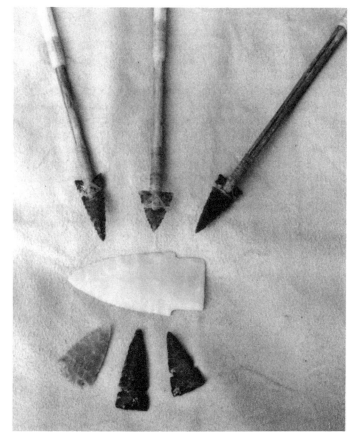

*Arrow heads around
white flint knife blade.*

"Bird Points" obsidian left, and flint.

antler, and allowing for occasional breakage, there are at least a couple of hours represented in each point.

Most original arrowheads are fairly small, 1½" by 3/4", or less. Ishi made some beautiful points almost 3" long, but this was not typical. In fact, the small so-called "bird-points" are, in my opinion, not for birds or small game at all, but for big game. The purpose of a point is to penetrate into the vital areas of a large animal, such as a buffalo or elk, and a small, thin, very sharp flint point penetrates much better than a wide chunky point. There are extremes, of course, but small points were used extensively on arrows since they penetrated well, were easier to make, and let the arrow fly better because they were lighter as well as having less wind resistance. Most of the hunting points I make are fairly small, less than 1½" long and about 5/8" wide, and have proven to be very deadly.

A few states have, for some irrational bureaucratic reason, outlawed flint and obsidian points by specifying that you can use only steel points for hunting. This logic is hard to follow since flint is as effective as steel and has been around fifty times as long. Perhaps the idea of our primitive origins is too

Stone points have proven to be just as effective as steel.

much for them to swallow, and they prefer to dictate that we use modern, progressive, expensive arrowheads. In most states, mine thankfully included, there is no restriction on the type of material, only on the dimensions of the point, which is quite reasonable.

Anyway, editorial opinion aside, flint points are beautiful and deadly if you're allowed to use them. I've talked with a number of other people who use flint points around the country, for everything from deer to bear to moose. I've never heard of an instance in which a flint point was placed in the engine room of an animal where the animal didn't cooperate and give up the ghost. I'm sure there are cases where an animal has been hit hard by a flint point and wasn't found, but seemingly to a lesser degree than with steel points or, for that matter, rifle bullets. Part of that may be due to the fact that anyone hardcore and backwards enough to hunt with wooden bows and flint points is going to be much better than average in the woods. They'll be, at the very least, a pretty good tracker and dedicated enough to stay with a wounded animal long after most hunters would have given up. I believe this explains why animals hit hard with flint points are almost always found.

There are a couple of different hafting techniques for flint arrowheads that involve some trade-offs. The side-notched point is easier to make but the notch in the wood shaft must be deeper to accept it. Making a deep notch in the wood is time consuming with flint tools but there is a way to make a point

Two methods of attaching flint points. The side notch, left, and the basal notch.

that takes a shallow notch. The only problem is, the basal notched flint point is more difficult to make, in that the notching process causes more failures because the corners of the point are weaker and easier to break. The trade-off is between an easier to make point and an easier to notch shaft.

BONE

Another natural material for arrowheads used occasionally was bone. I have seen a set of Kiowa arrows from the Southern Plains and a couple of arrows from the Northern Plains, as well as a few arrows from the East Coast tipped with bone. There have also been some recovered from archeological digs, such as at Cahokia, Illinois, and Pecos Pueblo, New Mexico. Bone points are not hard to make, but they are difficult to get very sharp. I haven't done any exhaustive study on this, but antelope leg bones seem to get considerably sharper than buffalo or deer. After the point is shaped and the edges thinned, it helps to get the edge of the point hot, which hardens the bone and enables it to take a better edge with a file or stone. Bone will make a useable point if it's all you have to work with, and it makes a pretty novelty point. It's durable, too, and won't usually break if a target is missed. For practical purposes, though, a good flint point is easier to make and is much sharper.

STEEL

When steel points became available they were quick to be used on Native American arrows. The flint points were effective but comparatively fragile and hard to make. If the steel points became bent on a bone or a rock, they were just hammered back to shape and resharpened. In most cases the Indians

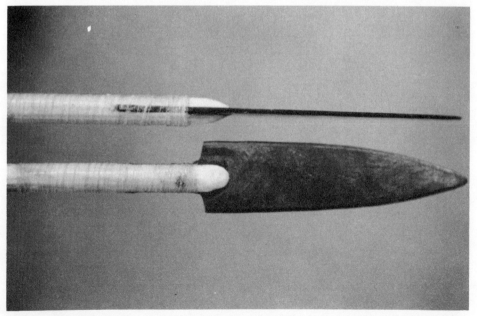

With any type of point, be sure to trim the leading edge of the shaft so it will penetrate cleanly.

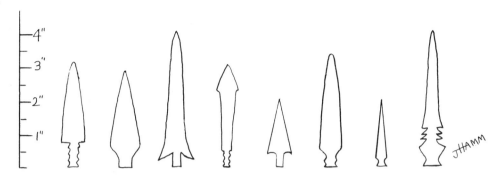

Original steel point designs.

didn't even have to make the steel points since the traders often supplied them ready-made. The Comanches, for instance, had been obtaining steel points from the Spanish in New Mexico since about the year 1700. The situation was much the same throughout the country, when the steel points became available, they were utilized. In some areas the steel points became predominate. Probably 98% of the hundreds of Plains arrows I have examined had metal points. The Comanches and Kiowas obtained many thousands from the Spanish, along with the tools and materials to make their own, so they soon gave up making them out of flint altogether. The Comanches quit making flint points so early that, to my knowledge, there has never been one identified as being made by them.

In other areas, however, the use of steel was not so overwhelming. On the West Coast, at least half of the arrows were tipped with flint and obsidian. In present day Yellowstone Park, in the 1830's, one observer wrote that the Shoshone Indians of the area had arrows that were all tipped with obsidian. About half of the Apache arrows from the Southwest I have observed were armed with flint points and the other half with steel. Many sets of arrows from the West Coast, the Southwest, and the East, are mixed, with part of the arrows in a quiver using flint heads and the rest using steel.

The Native Americans used steel points because they had some advantages, but they also held on to the ability to make their own from flint and obsidian. The steel points were often hard to get or long distances had to be covered to get to a trader. The ready-made points were expensive, too, for people who lived directly from the land. So while the steel points were used extensively, most groups kept the option of supplying themselves with points from available materials.

Some of the best material I've found to make my own steel points comes from the bands around heavy equipment tires. It's just the right thickness and is very springy. In order to cut it, you first have to detemper it, because it's so hard. Simply get it red-hot with an acetylene torch or put it into coals for a while. The metal will then be much easier to cut with snips or a chisel. When the basic shape is cut out, the point can be evened up and the edges thinned with a grinder or file. The steel is retempered after the point is made by getting it red hot once again and quenching it in oil or water.

A great many original steel points have rounded tips. I've been told by Native Americans that this was done so the point would glance off of an animal's bone and keep penetrating, rather than sticking into it. The theory makes sense, even though there is an ongoing argument to this day about whether a point should be rounded or sharpened to a needle tip. Original steel points were made both ways so take your pick.

I have seen some Cherokee arrows from the Southeast tipped with brass. The triangular points were cut out of brass kettles obtained from traders. You may not be aware that Native Americans were using metal points before Columbus arrived. I was surprised to discover that the Indians in the Great Lakes region were sometimes taking pieces of raw copper, hammering it flat, then cutting it into arrowheads. So if you want to use a REALLY traditional arrowhead, hammer out a copper point and hunt with it. Just don't let a bureaucrat see it.

Points, of any type, can be attached with hide glue and a sinew wrapping. As with fletching, the flat thin loin sinew works best for points. Hide glue offers the easiest way to attach points, but many tribes, especially on the West Coast and in the Southwest, used pitch glue extensively to attach flint and obsidian points. Pine or cedar pitch can be melted and added to a small amount of powdered charcoal, which helps keep the pitch from becoming brittle. The glue will be like stiff chewing gum when it is first made, and a small ball of it can be worked into the notch cut for the arrowhead. The stone point is pushed firmly into the pitch glue and then wrapped with moist sinew. Be sure to line up any point, whether flint, steel, or bone, so that it's not out of center on the arrow. A good way to do this is to spin the arrow slowly after the point is attached to see if it wobbles, then make any slight adjustments necessary before the glue and sinew start to dry.

Part 3

QUIVERS AND BOWCASES

The quivers devised by Native Americans to carry and protect their arrows ranged from utilitarian to elaborate pieces of art.

The utilitarian quivers were often just a tube made from animal skin with a carrying strap added. A quiver such as this was very attractive when made from an animal with beautiful fur. Animals that were used for this type of quiver were bobcat, fox, coyote, and, in at least one case I have seen, black bear cub. The predatory animals like these were preferred across the country, probably as much for the medicine of the hunting animal as for the beauty of the fur. A few quivers on the West Coast were fashioned from the head and necks of deer. These could have doubled as hunting decoys, as Ishi had a deer head stuffed with grass which he used to coax deer into arrow range. A simple animal skin or tanned buckskin quiver was used throughout the country.

Quivers were also manufactured from plant materials in different areas. One of these was found on the Northwest Coast, where they were made from pieces of cedar in the form of a hollowed out tube 36″ long. This type would protect the arrows from becoming crushed and would also be waterproof. A pre-historic Anasazi quiver was constructed of woven cotton cloth. Birchbark provided the material for yet another quiver from the Northeast. The bark was fashioned into a tube that would protect the arrows and be waterproof. This type of quiver had some fur, deer on the ones I have seen, around its mouth to protect the arrows and keep them from rattling around.

The most elaborate and highly decorated quivers came from the Plains area and were in reality a quiver and bow case combination. These were made by all of the Plains tribes along with Apaches, Utes, Shoshones, Nez Perce, Bannocks, and Flatheads. Some of the Missouri River area tribes made their quivers this way with a quiver and carrying strap, along with a tube of the same material for a bowcase. This was a handy way to carry the whole rig at one time especially on a horse. The preferred materials were brain-tanned buckskin, otter, mountain lion, lynx or bobcat, coyote, fox, and longhorn steer, approximately in that order.

To make a quiver and bowcase combination will require four otter or badger hides. An outfit can be made with three coyote or lynx hides. The single hide of a large mountain lion or mule deer will also make an entire quiver and bowcase.

If you're making a quiver from tanned hide, you'll probably want to line the soft skin with rawhide, so the sharp points won't pierce the hide. I use a tube of rawhide that is about two inches less than the total arrow length, since I like for the quiver to almost completely enclose and protect the arrows. The rawhide is 10″ across the bottom and 12″ across the top to allow a little more

*Ishi's otter skin quiver.
If a man used a short
bow it was often carried
in the quiver with the
arrows. Courtesy Lowie
Museum of Anthropology,
University of California at
Berkeley.*

room for feathers. The hide is folded into a teardrop shape which will keep the fletching from getting crushed, and a teardrop shaped end is sewn into the bottom to help keep the shape and to give the points some room. Also, glue or sew a thick piece of fur into the bottom of the quiver to protect the points especially if you're using flint.

These Plains quivers normally opened to the left and were worn on the back. The strap hung over the left shoulder across the chest and under the right arm. The reason for their opening to the left was so the strap could be switched to the right shoulder and the quiver placed under the left arm. This put the opening of the quiver forward on the left side. When chasing buffalo the Indians would ride up to where the animal was just ahead of them and to the left. The quiver placement made it handy to reach down on the same side and extract another arrow for a second or third shot.

The bowcase usually hung on top of the quiver, though I have seen a couple of examples where it hung underneath. It usually covered almost the entire

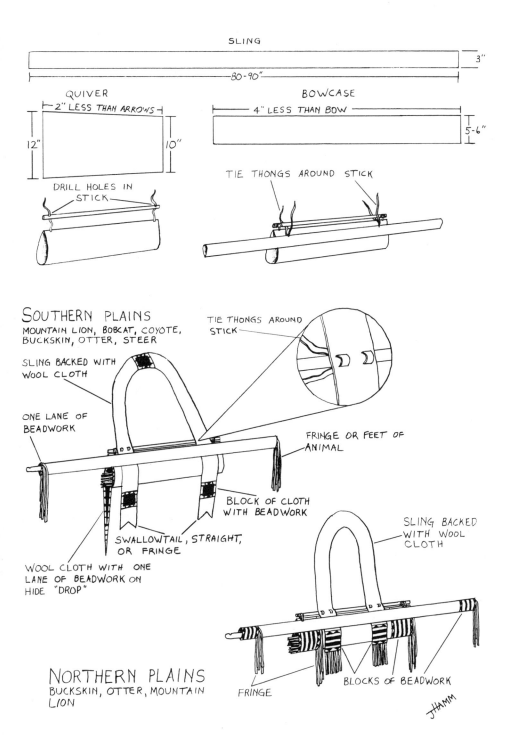

SLING

3"

80-90"

QUIVER

2" LESS THAN ARROWS

12" 10"

DRILL HOLES IN STICK

BOWCASE

4" LESS THAN BOW

5-6"

TIE THONGS AROUND STICK

SOUTHERN PLAINS
MOUNTAIN LION, BOBCAT, COYOTE, BUCKSKIN, OTTER, STEER

SLING BACKED WITH WOOL CLOTH

ONE LANE OF BEADWORK

TIE THONGS AROUND STICK

FRINGE OR FEET OF ANIMAL

BLOCK OF CLOTH WITH BEADWORK

SWALLOWTAIL, STRAIGHT, OR FRINGE

WOOL CLOTH WITH ONE LANE OF BEADWORK ON HIDE "DROP"

SLING BACKED WITH WOOL CLOTH

NORTHERN PLAINS
BUCKSKIN, OTTER, MOUNTAIN LION

FRINGE

BLOCKS OF BEADWORK

JHAMM

A Hidatsa man, from the northern plains, shows how a quiver and bowcase were carried. Courtesy Department of Library Services, American Museum of Natural History.

The same man shows how a quiver was worn under the left arm when ready for use from horseback. Note extra arrow held in the bow hand and the arrows held in the mouth. Courtesy Department of Library Services, American Museum of Natural History.

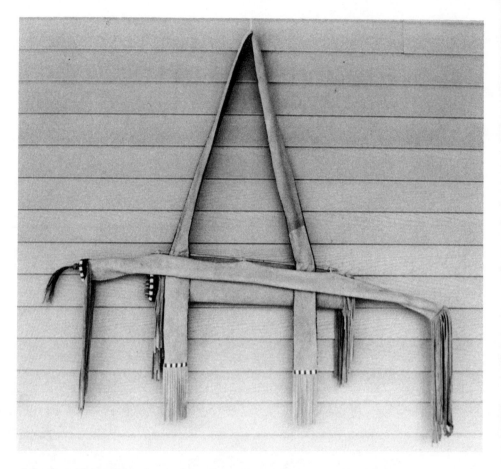

A Southern Plains-style quiver and bowcase made from brain-tanned buckskin.

bow, with only a couple of inches of wood left exposed. The ends of the bow-case were often fringed with the same type of hide. Another option is to sew the feet of the animal around the mouth of the bowcase, as was done with two bobcat feet on a Kiowa quiver I examined in the Field Museum in Chicago, and on a Comanche quiver made from mountain lion in the Milwaukee County Museum.

The quivers themselves were decorated in a number of different ways, depending on the time period and region of the Plains. Early on, the Northern quivers were decorated with quillwork, some elaborately so. Later, in the 1830's and 40's, the quillwork was supplanted by beadwork, though some Sioux quivers were decorated with a combination of quill and bead work up until the reservation period.

Many Plains quivers, both Northern and Southern, had a long triangular piece of hide sewn to the mouth of the quiver and up North sometimes to the bowcase, as well. This piece was from the same kind of animal as the rest of

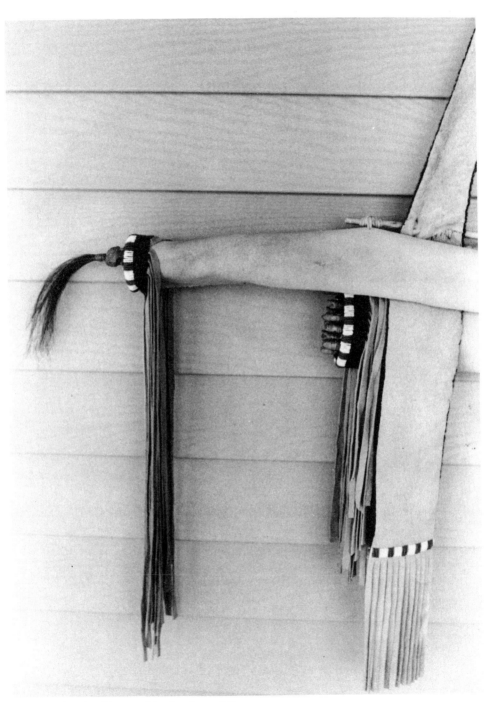

Close-up showing fringe and beadwork on cloth.

YAH-VI-NY,
COMANCHE LEA[

Comanche man wearing otter skin quiver with twisted buckskin fringe. Courtesy Ft. Sill Museum.

the outfit, and hung down gracefully below the quiver. In the North, this "drop," or "drops" if also placed on the bowcase, was usually fully beaded. The Nez Perce and Crow were famous for these spectacular beaded otterhide quivers. On the Southern Plains, the drop was placed only on the quiver and was not fully beaded, but had the flesh side of the hide covered with cloth, usually red. The edges of the cloth had a row of beadwork applied. Down the center of the triangular strip of cloth were placed small brass bells, or brass buttons, or brass tacks holding short pieces of brightly colored ribbon. A Southern quiver like this usually had a piece of red cloth around the mouth of the bowcase, as well, with a single lane of beadwork on it. I have seen quivers like this made from brain-tanned buckskin, mountain lion, bobcat, and longhorn steer.

A Northern Plains-style otter quiver with "drops" hanging from the mouth of the quiver and the bowcase. The flesh side of the otter skin drops are covered with red wool cloth and the edge of the cloth is beaded. Note the wide piece of cloth extending beyond the fur sling and the fur fringe bundles, with beadwork, hanging from the ends of the drops and attached to the sling. Photo by David Wright.

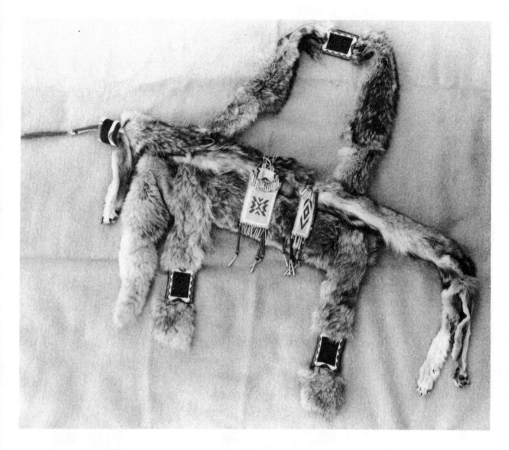

A Southern Plains-style quiver and bowcase made from coyote. Note the beadwork on the cloth panels, the coyote feet and legs used instead of fringe, and the beaded bags for flint and steel fire-making tools and an awl. This exceptional quiver was made by Barry Hardin.

The strap was generally about 3" wide and 80" to 90" long, and passed between the bowcase and the quiver. Six inches to a foot of the strap hung down below the quiver. This section of the strap sometimes had a square piece of red cloth sewn on it with a lane of beadwork around the outside edge of the cloth. The strap is attached to a stick, about arrowshaft size and the length of the quiver, which is used to anchor the quiver and bow case together. You won't want the quiver to hang too low, but at about waist height, so adjust it on the sling accordingly.

Many of the men on the Southern Plains carried beaded pouches on their quivers that were much like those worn by women on their belts. In fact, for a long time I was convinced that the beaded pouches shown in early studio pictures were photographers' props, and did not really belong on the quivers. However, I have seen so many of these, by so many different photographers,

A Kiowa man with mountain lion quiver ca. 1870. Note the beaded bags for firemaking tools and awl. Courtesy Western History Collections, University of Oklahoma Library.

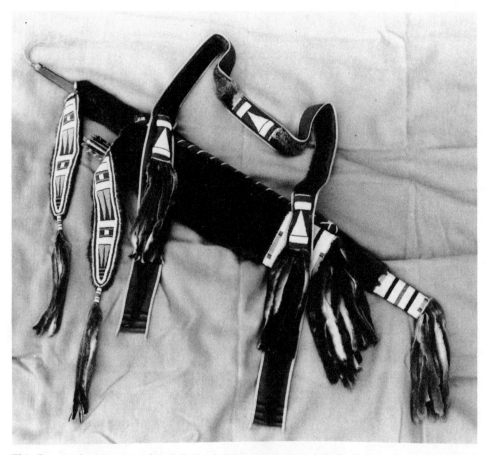

This Crow-style otter quiver has fully beaded drops as well as fully beaded panels on the ends of the quiver and bowcase. This striking quiver was made by Don Walske.

that I am convinced the men carried beaded cases similar, if not identical, to the ones worn on a woman's belt. There were usually two cases, a flat one for flint and steel and tinder, and a round one for an awl. This remains a good way to carry these necessary tools.

Part 4

SHOOTING

Now that all the time, effort, failures, sweat, and imaginative language are behind you comes the fun part, shooting the weapons that were made with your own hands. Traditional bows and arrows made from wood and sinew can perform just as well as modern laminated recurves and longbows, as some chronograph tests described earlier prove out. Don't be disappointed, though, if your first bow doesn't shoot at rocket-like speeds. Don't be disappointed in it at all, as long as it shoots and you learned from it. Remember, there is no such animal as the perfect bow. Recently, at a large traditional archery tournament in Michigan, Jay Massey, John Strunk, Ron Hardcastle, and I gave a seminar on making self bows and sinew-backed bows to about 250 people. Someone in the audience asked a question about making the ultimate bow, and the four of us, who have probably made upwards of a thousand bows, laughingly admitted that none of us had ever yet made the perfect bow, though we all intend to keep trying. So don't be discouraged if your first bow is not exactly what you wanted, take what you learned from it and build on that.

Everyone who makes his own bow develops a shooting style that works best for him. You may have tailored the bow to use a standard anchor point and release, with three fingers wrapped around the string and the arrow held between index and middle fingers. This is the way I shoot, since I grew up with it and have difficulty using some of the Indian-style releases, such as the unorthodox method that Ishi used.

I had always wondered how some of the short Plains bows could be unbacked and not break when pulled with an arrow that was half its length. While closely watching some Comanche men shooting their traditional 48" bows with 24" arrows, I discovered the answer. They held the raised nock of the arrow between thumb and forefinger, with the middle and ring fingers resting on the string. These men shoot instinctively, with no anchor point, and push the bow as much as pull the arrow. They shoot in one fluid motion, as the bow is pushed forward the arrow hand comes toward the upper chest and the arrow is released. With the pinch-type grip they use, it is almost impossible to pull a strong bow to full draw, so when the force of the bow reaches a certain point, as it's pushed forward, the arrow is automatically pulled from between the fingers. I watched them at length before realizing that they weren't pulling the arrow back all the way, that they were probably drawing 20". That is why their bows didn't have to be backed.

The Comanche archers usually hold three or four more arrows in the bow hand, points up, and can immediately pull another arrow upward through the grip, nock it, and send it on its way in one quick motion. Their shooting looks

A Kiowa man, Koyei, demonstrates the pinch grip used on plains arrows with a raised nock. Note extra arrows held in bow hand with the points up. Courtesy Western History Collections, University of Oklahoma Library.

strange to one brought up with anchor points and classic English shooting styles. That is, until you glance down at the target and notice that at fifteen yards their arrows are in a fist-sized group. No way would I shoot against them, strange style or not, if there was any money involved.

One of the most enjoyable ways to shoot, and which for me gives the very best practice, is to rove in the field and shoot at targets of opportunity, leaves, sticks, rabbits, small rocks, squirrels, and so forth. The only drawback to this theory is that if you're using handmade arrows, which I like to do, you destroy or lose a lot of them. In the last ten years it seems like I've lost right at a million dollars worth of arrows. At least, when it takes half a day to make one arrow it seems like it. A wonderful solution to the problem is a point like the Judo, if it doesn't offend your sense of aesthetics. It sure doesn't offend mine, since these sturdy little points have protruding wires which prevent them from skipping under the grass and getting lost. They're also nearly unbreakable and are death on small game. They can be ordered with a socket to fit on a wooden arrow and I use them with dogwood shafts. The Judo points aren't cheap, something like $5.00 a pop, but compared to a million dollars worth of arrows they're a steal.

Apache hunters ca. 1870. The kneeling man is left-handed. Courtesy Smithsonian Institute.

Ishi using his unorthodox, but effective, shooting technique ca. 1914. Courtesy Lowie Museum of Anthropology, University of California at Berkely.

Wandering about shooting at different targets is good practice for actual hunting. The targets you shoot are at different angles and unknown ranges. When you've shot a particular bow for awhile, you naturally begin to adjust to the distances and allow for them automatically. The handmade bow, after a couple of thousand shots, becomes an extension of your arm and you'll surprise yourself with the shots you can make.

When a bow is not in use, it should always be unstrung. It can be laid flat across two pegs in the wall or hung by putting the unstrung loop over a nail. Another good way to store a bow is to put it in a bowcase and quiver that is hung on the wall. Don't ever stand the bow in a corner since it may warp.

On a hunting trip it has become a habit for me to unstring a sinew-backed bow and place it in the sun any time I'm not using it. Before taking a sinew-backed bow out to shoot it, remember that a couple of hours spent in the sun will make it shoot better.

Something to be aware of with osage orange is that it will darken with age. It is a bright, gaudy yellow when first worked but will turn nearly black after twenty or thirty years. The wood will begin to darken within a year or so, and I'm convinced that it's the sunlight that causes it. At least, with a bow that is kept in a bowcase with only a few inches exposed to the light, the exposed portion will get dark while the rest of the bow will remain a bright yellow. This darkening process doesn't harm the bow and in fact adds character to it.

Be very judicious about letting people unfamiliar with traditional weapons handle your bow. I've had people bend them backwards across their knee, attempt to draw a 48" bow 30", and try to string them backwards, among other mishaps. I haven't made but a couple of enemies over it, but the point is, supervise anyone who wants to examine your bow, or the bow and the friendship may come to grief.

When you make a bow that's what you want, stick with it. One of my downfalls, as a shooter, is that I'm always shooting a different bow, either checking one out for a customer before it's shipped or trying a new style for myself. I'd undoubtedly be a lot better off if I picked a bow and stuck with it. When I finish a bow it usually seems that it would be better if it was just a little shorter, longer, stronger, weaker, had more recurve, setback, speed, or something. Never being satisfied makes for a good bowyer. Really expecting to build a perfect bow makes for ulcers.

Even if there are some things about your bow that you would change, you coaxed it into existence and there isn't another one like it. When you get to where you shoot it well, or hunt and take game with it, there comes a true satisfaction like no other.

The author in his "invisible" buckskin clothing.

BOWS AND ERRORS

I'm invisible. At least I hope so. I'd better be, since I plan to get within arrow range of a whitetail deer. Perched twenty feet up in this live oak tree in the Texas Hill Country, I start to slow down and blend in after the long hike up the canyon. As a full-time bowmaker and volunteer historian, I spend a lot of time in the woods recreating the conditions that early people faced in order to learn about their way of life. It always seems that I have to suffer before any of the knowledge sinks in, witness this trip the three of us have taken to attempt to live as Stone-Age people had. Bringing nothing but what we have made by hand, we plan to survive with what our ingenuity and skill can provide. After four days I'm beginning to wonder if we haven't miscalculated and won't starve to death.

I select a dogwood arrow and nock it on my osage orange bow as I lean against the trunk to wait. Some people harrass me unmercifully for using these old-time Indian-style weapons, but I figure if wooden bows and flint points worked for a few thousand years they should still work. Besides, the compound bows the critics use are like carrying bicycles through the woods, so their sniping doesn't bother me much.

Turkeys begin to talk to each other up and down the draw. It must be the same bunch I flushed on the edge of the canyon, when they exploded out of the cedars like a covey of quail right at my feet. I recovered from that heart attack and now hope to get even as the scattered birds cluck to each other. I'm in luck as two turkeys run towards my tree and I get ready, balanced like a circus performer on a big branch, to make a trick shot. The birds run by within twenty yards so I fling an arrow at one through a small opening in the branches and watch, in slow motion, the turkey and arrow arriving at the same time. As the turkey rolls, I'm thinking, "Wow, what a shot!", but the bird immediately is up running again and the arrow is left stuck in the ground. It gradually dawns on me that the arrow must have struck inches in front of the turkey, and since he was running and never saw it, he tripped over the shaft and went sprawling. I laugh out loud at gaining revenge and decide to tell my companions that anybody can kill a turkey, but it takes real skill to humiliate one. They'll probably fail to see the humor in it and would prefer I brought back something to eat.

Food has been surprisingly hard to come by on this trip. Finding buffalo nonexistent for some reason, and the deer way too smart for us, we've had to be content for the last five days with one rattlesnake, four perch, and a handful of crawdads. In this part of Texas there are usually lots of edible plants and we've been foraging for cattail, dried persimmons, walnuts, and a few pecans. It's late in the fall, though, and most of the edibles are about gone. The food intake has been something less than adequate, and it's beginning to occur to me why the Indians had such a universal reputation for toughness.

A shallow cave in a cliff face provides shelter and we start our fires with friction, literally by rubbing two yucca stalks together. A beautiful spring splashes out just down the slope so with shelter and fire all of our basic needs are taken care of — except for food.

Yesterday had been promising, and we were starting to think we might make Journeyman cavemen. A big mistake. Mark had decided to try for more fish, and John wanted to check his deadfalls and snares. All of us were getting lightheaded and a little weak from the lack of food and constant exercise, so we had agreed to meet back at camp in the afternoon to eat whatever had been caught. I headed down the canyon to try once again to arrow the rabbit that I had gotten to be on first name terms with, but after two hours of stalking about friend cottontail was unfortunately nowhere to be found.

I dug and sampled some cattail roots and they were quite bland, unlike most wild edibles which are bitter, but they didn't excite me much since I was used to peppers and cheese and flavor enhancers (all carcinogenic, of course, but cancer wouldn't kill me as fast as this starvation would).

Lying down under a bush with the beginnings of a headache, I hoped fervently that someone else had killed something. When you're ravenously hungry a weakness takes hold that is impossible to talk yourself out of so I closed my eyes to rest up for the trip back to camp.

Through the haze of sleepiness I suddenly realized I could hear something coming towards me out of the brush and sat up to get the bow ready. Desperately wanting a deer, when I saw movement I drew back the arrow and watched a slow elk step into the open at about ten yards. He turned and looked at me while I was concentrating on the spot just back from his shoulder where the flint arrowhead would go. I gradually relaxed the bow and the slow elk said "Mooooo" and turned and trotted off, unaware how close he came to meeting his Maker. We have permission to be here, but I figured it was judicious not to shoot the rancher's Hereford.

Getting to my feet, I grabbed the bush as a rush of dizziness passed. I had a big headache but it was nothing that about a gallon of lasagne wouldn't cure. I picked a hatful of cattails on the way back to camp, still hoping that the others were more successful in the day's hunt. My prayers were answered, for when I got back Mark and John were concentrating on the pot boiling in a big fire.

"What did you get?," I wanted to know.

"I got two fish and John got a rabbit," Mark allowed with a large grin.

"No luck," I said, and started cutting up the cattails and throwing them in the pot while I told them about the Hereford. They both seemed a little disappointed that I didn't shoot it. Mark told us about his death-defying skill in sneaking up on the fish and spearing them, and we congratulated him on not dying before he could bring back the food. The meal boiled for another twenty minutes and when we finally couldn't stand it anymore, John and I started manuevering the pot out of the fire. Fate did not smile upon us for as we moved the pot it fell upside down from the flaming log where it had been sitting and dumped the contents into the fire. We stared stupidly at our first real meal in four days being absorbed by the ashes.

"Let me put it this way," Mark said, and gave a short treatise on animal by-products.

I couldn't have agreed more, and was beginning to consider suicide when Mark started giggling. I looked up at him sharply as John began to laugh, too. It was contagious, and we were soon all on the ground doubled up with laughter. After recovering we felt a little better and could forget our aching hunger, sort of.

With some daylight still left, we took our bows and spread out again to search for something to eat. I hunted until almost dark, missing a rabbit and a bunch of quail, before starting back up the canyon. When nearly to camp I came to a big fire with a half-dozen people sitting around it. They must have just come into the canyon because when I went through there three hours before the place was deserted. I eased up close to them in the darkness and stood, just at the edge of the firelight, and noticed that they had several ice chests, which was amazing since we were at least two brutal miles from a road and half of the people were women.

I felt, rather than saw, Mark moving slowly up to my left and we stood, unobserved, as they began to take food and drinks out of their coolers. I was trying to make up my mind whether to go for the women or the potato salad first when John walked up just inside the firelight on the far side of the fire. One of the girls saw him and jumped to her feet with a start. The three men and three women looked about at John and Mark and me; we smelled like burning javelinas and were drooling like mad dogs at the mountain of food in their camp. Have I mentioned that you get stupendously dirty on a trip like this? After five days out here I look like I've been living under a bridge for five months, little wonder that we were getting such alarmed looks.

Ever the statesman, I broke the silence and asked if they would trade a sandwich for a pickup. Mark grabbed a handful of my buckskin shirt and pulled me into the darkness. John saw us leave and ducked behind a rock, leaving the bewildered campers looking about nervously in the firelight, wondering what on earth was going on.

On the way back to our cave, I reminded my tough, hardcore companions that we still didn't have anything to eat. Take what nature provides, that's my motto, but Mark sternly insisted that nature doesn't provide potato salad and beer . . .

The sun is getting close to the horizon as a few small birds flit around my live oak tree. I'm trying hard not to think about my growling stomach. We've had nothing to eat since day before yesterday, and I'm watching patiently for the Hereford. I've seen three deer today, two does and a small buck, but they were all out of my twenty-five yard bow range.

I enjoy watching the natural world through the cloak of invisibility, and have been completely entertained throughout the afternoon by deer and birds and squirrels and clouds and trees, but especially by migrating Monarch butterflies, hundreds of which have interrupted their long flight to Mexico by stopping for the night in my tree. I've only seen their colorful mass parade once before, years ago, and the sight alone was worth the trip.

The full moon is overhead and I feel a bit guilty because most of the time, living in a house, I'm not sure what phase it's in, though it's something important that one should know. Living outside, the moon phase is absorbed by osmosis; you're always aware of it because it helps determine the movement of animals, the feeding cycles of fish, the lunacy of your companions, the stealthy, murderous approach of aborigines . . .

I'm snatched back from my daydream as a doe materializes from thin air and trots into the open, fifteen yards away. The bow somehow draws itself and an arrow appears in the side of the deer, a big surprise to both me and her. She crashes through the brush, bounces off of a tree, then disappears. I resist the temptation to jump screaming out of the tree to give chase, instead remaining still for twenty minutes to give the razor sharp flint point time to do its age-old work.

She has gone less than thirty yards. When I finally kneel down beside her the emotion of the kill, a strange tangle of delight and sadness, floods through me. Placing a pinch of tobacco on the ground, I thank the deer for joining me and promise to use her body well, to use not only the meat but the sinew, bones, hooves, and hide.

After gutting the deer and performing an autopsy I start dragging her back to camp. The doe is not all that big, but by the time I've drug her nearly a mile to the rock shelter it's dark and I'm beginning to wonder if I'm not dragging the Hereford.

Elation rules the camp when I bring in the deer. The scene could easily be from five thousand years ago, when the hungry people applaud the hunter as they realize that they aren't going to starve just yet. We hang the deer from a tree, and place fresh tenderloin and backstrap steaks on sticks just above the coals.

John accuses me of rank luck in making the kill. When that gets no response, Mark muses about what fence I found the doe hung in, but I just smile and gesture toward the deer hanging at the edge of the firelight, as if to ask, "Where's yours?" They laugh with great good humor when they see there's no way to insult me tonight.

While waiting for our venison steaks to get done, we tell the usual incredible stories, some made all the more incredible by the fact that there is some truth to them. The firelight reflects from the overhanging rock wall, giving us a timeless security as the firewood releases its long stored heat from the sun. Camaraderie around the open fire seems luxurious as we drink in the delicious smell of cooking meat. When the food is finally passed around, I decide it feels good to bring meat to camp and share the stories of the hunt. The feeling is an all too rare one of competence and accomplishment, and though it must be older than dirt, it sits well on a space-age man and I soak it up like heat from the fire. The meat is the best I've ever tasted.

REFERENCES

BOOKS
Duval, John C., The Adventures of Bigfoot Wallace, University of Nebraska
Press, 1966.
Elmer, Robert P., Target Archery, Alfred A. Knopf, 1946.
Flint Institute of Arts, The Art of the Great Lakes Indians, 1973.
Heizer, Robert F., and Kroeber, Theodora, Ishi the Last Yahi - a Documentary
History, University of California Press, 1979.
Klopsteg, Paul E., Turkish Archery and the Composite Bow, Private Printing,
1947.
Kroeber, Theodora, Ishi in Two Worlds, University of California Press, 1961.
Mason, Otis Tufton, North American Bows, Arrows, and Quivers,
Smithsonian Annual Report, 1893.
Massey, Jay, The Bowyer's Craft, Bear Paw Publications, 1987.
Peckham, Stewart, Prehistoric Weapons in the Southwest, The Museum of
New Mexico Press, 1965.
Pope, Saxton T., Bows and Arrows, University of California Press, 1962.
Powell, Father Peter John, People of the Sacred Mountain, A History of the
Northern Cheyenne Chiefs and Warrior Societies 1830-1879, Harper and
Row, 1975.
Russell, Osborne, Journal of a Trapper, University of Nebraska Press, 1965.
Stewart, Hilary, Cedar-Tree of Life to the Northwest Coast Indians, University
of Washington Press, 1984.
Strong, Emory, Stone Age in the Great Basin, Binford and Mort, 1969.

PERIODICALS

American Indian Art, Axel Schulze-Thulin, Prairie and Plains Collections of
the Linden-Museum Stuttgart, Summer, 1979.
American Antiquity, Frank C. Hibben, Old Bow Cache From the Mogollon
Mountain, July, 1938.
Bowman Review, M. H. Brumble, Some Observations on Osage, June, 1946.